Edexcel GCSE (9-1)

History

Mao's China, 1945–1976

Series Editor: Angela Leonard   Author: Robin Bunce

ALWAYS LEARNING   **PEARSON**

Published by Pearson Education Limited, 80 Strand, London, WC2R 0RL.

www.pearsonschoolsandfecolleges.co.uk

Copies of official specifications for all Edexcel qualifications may be found on the website: www.edexcel.com

Text © Pearson Education Limited 2017

Series editor: Angela Leonard
Designed by Colin Tilley Loughrey, Pearson Education Limited
Typeset by Phoenix Photosetting, Chatham, Kent
Original illustrations © Pearson Education Limited
Illustrated by KJA Artists Illustration Agency and Phoenix Photosetting, Chatham, Kent.

Cover design by Colin Tilley Loughrey
Cover photo © Bridgeman Art Library Ltd: National Portrait Gallery, London, UK

The right of Robin Bunce to be identified as author of this work has been asserted by her in accordance with the Copyright, Designs and Patents Act 1988.

First published 2017

British Library Cataloguing in Publication Data
A catalogue record for this book is available from the British Library.
ISBN 978 1 292 12735 4

A note from the publisher
In order to ensure that this resource offers high-quality support for the associated Pearson qualification, it has been through a review process by the awarding body. This process confirms that this resource fully covers the teaching and learning content of the specification or part of a specification at which it is aimed. It also confirms that it demonstrates an appropriate balance between the development of subject skills, knowledge and understanding, in addition to preparation for assessment.

Endorsement does not cover any guidance on assessment activities or processes (e.g. practice questions or advice on how to answer assessment questions), included in the resource nor does it prescribe any particular approach to the teaching or delivery of a related course.

While the publishers have made every attempt to ensure that advice on the qualification and its assessment is accurate, the official specification and associated assessment guidance materials are the only authoritative source of information and should always be referred to for definitive guidance.

Pearson examiners have not contributed to any sections in this resource relevant to examination papers for which they have responsibility.

Examiners will not use endorsed resources as a source of material for any assessment set by Pearson.

Endorsement of a resource does not mean that the resource is required to achieve this Pearson qualification, nor does it mean that it is the only suitable material available to support the qualification, and any resource lists produced by the awarding body shall include this and other appropriate resources.

Websites
Pearson Education Limited is not responsible for the content of any external internet sites. It is essential for tutors to preview each website before using it in class so as to ensure that the URL is still accurate, relevant and appropriate. We suggest that tutors bookmark useful websites and consider enabling students to access them through the school/college intranet.

Contents

How to use this book

What's covered?

This book covers the Modern Depth study on Mao's China, 1945–76. This unit makes up 30% of your GCSE course, and will be examined in Paper 3.

Modern depth studies cover a short period of time, and require you to know about a society or historical situation in detail. You need to understand different aspects within this period, such as social, economic, political, cultural and military aspects, and how they interact with each other. This book also explains the different types of exam questions you will need to answer, and includes advice and example answers to help you improve.

Features

As well as a clear, detailed explanation of the key knowledge you will need, you will also find a number of features in the book:

Key terms

Where you see a word followed by an asterisk, like this: Militia*, you will be able to find a Key Terms box on that page that explains what the word means.

> **Key term**
>
> **Propaganda***
>
> Publications and media designed to promote a persuasive political message.

Activities

Every few pages, you'll find a box containing some activities designed to help check and embed knowledge and get you to really think about what you've studied. The activities start simple, but might get more challenging as you work through them.

Summaries and Checkpoints

At the end of each chunk of learning, the main points are summarised in a series of bullet points – great for embedding the core knowledge, and handy for revision.

Checkpoints help you to check and reflect on your learning. The Strengthen section helps you to consolidate knowledge and understanding, and check that you've grasped the basic ideas and skills. The Challenge questions push you to go beyond just understanding the information, and into evaluation and analysis of what you've studied.

Sources and Interpretations

This book contains numerous contemporary pictorial and text sources that show what people from the period, said, thought or created.

The book also includes extracts from the work of historians, showing how experts have interpreted the events you've been studying.

You will need to be comfortable examining both sources and interpretations to answer questions in your Paper 3 exam.

> **Source E**
>
> A government poster created in 1960 by the CCP. The text says 'Getting organised is boundlessly good'.

> **Interpretation 1**
>
> From *The Cambridge History of China* by Denis Twitchett and John K. Fairbank, published in 1991.
>
> His [Mao's] personal authority gave him enough power to unleash potent social forces, but not enough power to control them. And his confidence that the masses … would be the salvation of the country proved woefully misplaced as the mass movement degenerated into violence, factionalism, and chaos. The Cultural Revolution … became the monumental error of his latter years.

Extend your knowledge

These features contain useful additional information that adds depth to your knowledge, and to your answers. The information is closely related to the key issues in the unit, and questions are sometimes included, helping you to link the new details to the main content.

> **Extend your knowledge**
>
> **Zhou Enlai**
>
> As a university student in the 1920s, Zhou travelled across Europe. He worked with the CCP from the time he returned to China in 1924. Following the Chinese Revolution, Zhou played a key role in government. As Mao's foreign minister he established good relations with countries in Africa and Latin America, such as Tanzania, Peru and Mexico. He was Mao's main ally in rebuilding the CCP after 1969. He was a genuinely popular politician. Indeed, on his death in 1976, crowds of mourners filled Tiananmen Square, leading to protests against radicals in the government.

Exam-style questions and tips

The book also includes extra exam-style questions you can use to practise. These appear in the chapters and are accompanied by a tip to help you get started on an answer.

Exam-style question, Section B

How useful are Sources H and I for an enquiry into the purpose of the *Laogai* system? Explain your answer, using Sources H and I and your knowledge of the historical context. **8 marks**

Exam tip

When analysing and evaluating the utility of the sources you do not need to reach a judgement about which of the sources is more useful.

Recap pages

At the end of each chapter, you'll find a page designed to help you to consolidate and reflect on the chapter as a whole. Each recap page includes a recall quiz, ideal for quickly checking your knowledge or for revision. Recap pages also include activities designed to help you summarise and analyse what you've learned, and also reflect on how each chapter links to other parts of the unit.

THINKING HISTORICALLY

These activities are designed to help you develop a better understanding of how history is constructed, and are focused on the key areas of Evidence, Interpretations, Cause & Consequence and Change & Continuity. In the Modern Depth Study, you will come across activities on Cause & Consequence, Evidence and Interpretations as these are key areas of focus for this unit.

The Thinking Historically approach has been developed in conjunction with Dr Arthur Chapman and the Institute of Education, UCL. It is based on research into the misconceptions that can hold students back in history.

THINKING HISTORICALLY Cause and Consequence (3c&d) — conceptual map reference

The Thinking Historically conceptual map can be found at: www.pearsonschools.co.uk/thinkinghistoricallygcse

At the end of most chapters is a spread dedicated to helping you improve your writing skills. These include simple techniques you can use in your writing to make your answers clearer, more precise and better focused on the question you're answering.

The Writing Historically approach is based on the *Grammar for Writing* pedagogy developed by a team at the University of Exeter and popular in many English departments. Each spread uses examples from the preceding chapter, so it's relevant to what you've just been studying.

Preparing for your exams

At the back of the book, you'll find a special section dedicated to explaining and exemplifying the new Edexcel GCSE History exams. Advice on the demands of this paper, written by Angela Leonard, helps you prepare for and approach the exam with confidence. Each question type is explained through annotated sample answers at two levels, showing clearly how answers can be improved.

Pearson Progression Scale: This icon indicates the Step that a sample answer has been graded at on the Pearson Progression Scale.

This book is also available as an online ActiveBook, which can be licensed for your whole institution.

There is also an ActiveLearn Digital Service available to support delivery of this book, featuring a front-of-class version of the book, lesson plans, worksheets, exam practice PowerPoints, assessments, notes on Thinking Historically and Writing Historically, and more.

ActiveLearn Digital Service

Timeline: Mao's China, 1945–76

Political

1946
Renewal of fighting in the Civil War

1948
CCP conquers Manchuria

1949
CCP victory in the Huai–Hai Campaign

1949
Foundation of the People's Republic of China

1950
Invasion of Tibet

1951
Launch of the 'three antis' movement

1952
Launch of the 'five antis' movement

1950
China enters Korean War

1950
Resist America, Aid Korea campaign begins

1955
Propaganda campaign against Hu Feng

1956
Launch of the Hundred Flowers campaign

1957
Mao's speech 'On the correct handling of contradictions among the people'

1957
'Anti-Rightist' purge

1959
Lushan Conference and purge of Peng Dehuai

1960
Liu Shaoqi and Deng Xiaoping adopt pragmatic economic policies

1945	1946	1947	1948	1949	1950	1951	1952	1953	1954	1955	1956	1957	1958	1959	1960

1950
Attacks on landlords

1950
Agrarian Reform Law

1950
Marriage Law

1951–52
Mutual Aid Teams introduced

1952
First Five-Year Plan developed

1953–54
Agricultural Producers' Co-operatives (APCs) introduced

1955–56
Advanced Agricultural Producers' Co-operatives (Advanced APCs) introduced

1957
Four Pests Campaign

1958
Great Leap Forward (second Five-Year Plan) begins

1958
Communes introduced

1958
Lysenkoism introduced

1958
Pinyin officially adopted

1958–62
Great famine

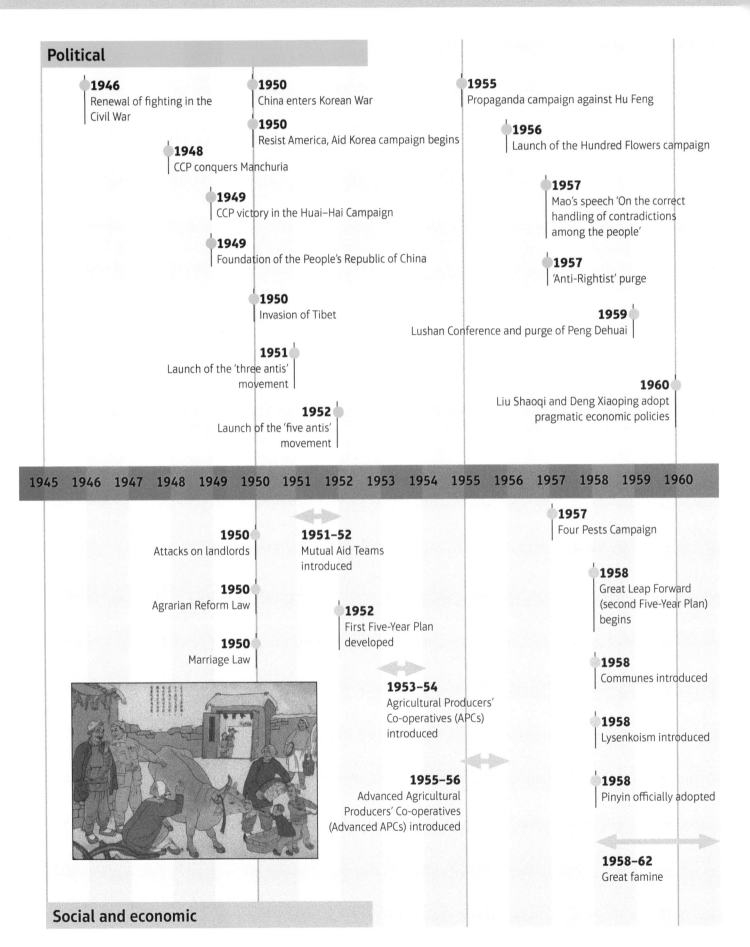

Social and economic

6

1963
Cult of Lei Feng

1969
Lin Biao named as
Mao's successor

1973
Deng Xiaoping returns to
government

1965
Mao's Twenty-Three Articles

1971
Lin Biao dies in
aeroplane crash

1976
Death of Zhou Enlai

1966
Cultural Revolution Group formed

1976
Deng Xiaoping removed
from government

1966
Red Guards form

1976
Death of Mao

1966
Mass rallies in Tiananmen Square

1976
Arrest of the
'Gang of Four'

1966
Deng Xiaoping and Liu Shaoqi
purged from government

1961	1962	1963	1964	1965	1966	1967	1968	1969	1970	1971	1972	1973	1974	1975	1976

1962
Industrial production
begins to recover

1968
Pinyin officially adopted by National
People's Congress

1963
Socialist Education
Movement launched

1968
'Up to the mountains and down to
the villages' campaign begins

1964
'Little Red Book' published for PLA

1964
Introduction of dwarf rice

1966
Cultural Revolution begins

1966
Mass distribution of the 'Little Red Book'

1966
'Four olds' campaign launched

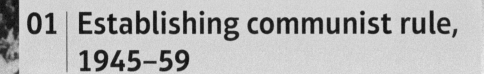

01 | Establishing communist rule, 1945–59

Between 1945 and 1959, China went through a period of dramatic change. In 1946, shortly after the end of the Second World War, China was again engulfed by full-scale civil war. The nationalist Guomindang (GMD), led by Chiang Kai-shek, attacked the Chinese Communist Party (CCP) in the north of China. Initially, the GMD gained ground. However, during 1949, the CCP defeated the GMD government. Mao Zedong (also spelled Tse-Tung in English), undisputed leader of the CCP, proclaimed the creation of the People's Republic of China (PRC) in October 1949.

From 1949 to 1950, Mao's new communist government worked with government officials and factory owners who had previously opposed them. However, during 1951 and 1952, Mao attacked supporters of the previous government and gained greater control over China's government and economy.

Mao's most radical policy in the early years of his rule was the Hundred Flowers campaign. This was a brief period of freedom in which intellectuals and students were encouraged to criticise the government. However, Mao quickly lost control of the campaign. Consequently, Mao started the 'Anti-Rightist' purge, a terror campaign against those who had spoken out against the government.

By 1959, the CCP's government was secure and Mao was the undisputed ruler of China.

Learning outcomes

In this chapter you will find out about:

- why Mao and the CCP won the Civil War
- Mao's key ideas
- how Mao governed China in the years 1949–59
- what happened during the 'antis' movements and the Hundred Flowers campaign.

1.1 The Civil War, 1945–49

After the Second World War, China experienced a devastating civil war. By 1949, the nationalist* Guomindang (GMD) government had lost and the Chinese Communist* Party (CCP) had won. Communist victory was brought about by their relative strengths, their tactics, popular support and foreign help.

Key terms

Nationalist*

Person or group who fights for the independence of their nation. It is important to remember that Mao and the CCP were also nationalists.

Communist*

Person or group who wants to end exploitation and establish a society in which everyone is equal. Communists fight for the rights of working people, particularly urban workers.

The relative strengths and weaknesses of the CCP and GMD in 1945

In 1945, as the Second World War ended, the GMD appeared to be much stronger than Mao Zedong's CCP.

GMD strengths

In 1945, the GMD had a number of strengths.

- It was the official government of China. As the official government, the GMD received help from other countries, such as the USA.
- It controlled most of China's major cities. As a result, the GMD controlled factories and could produce weapons, vehicles and other essential goods.
- It controlled the most densely populated parts of China. Therefore, the GMD controlled around 75% of the population.

- Its army totalled 2.5 million soldiers, twice the number of Mao's communist army, the People's Liberation Army (PLA).
- It had some popular support. Some citizens believed that Chiang was responsible for China's victory in the Second World War.
- The USA gave the GMD economic and military aid, as the USA did not want the CCP to control China.

Source A

Chiang Kai-shek representing China at the Cairo Conference of Allied Powers, alongside US president Franklin D. Roosevelt and British prime minister Winston Churchill. The photograph was taken in Cairo in 1943 by an American press photographer.

GMD weaknesses

At the same time, the GMD had a number of weaknesses, which undermined its chances of victory.

- Its failure to improve working conditions in factories meant that it was slowly losing working-class support.
- It had done little to enforce women's rights. For this reason, it lost support from many women and feminists* as time went on.
- It refused to allow land reform that would more fairly distribute the land. As a result, the GMD lost support among the peasants*.
- It introduced censorship*: therefore, it lost support, particularly among students.
- The corruption* of GMD officials and GMD economic policies led to unemployment and inflation*.

These failings became more obvious over time. Therefore, the GMD lost support as the Civil War went on.

Key terms

Feminists*

People whose central value is gender (sexual) equality, and who seek to achieve this by empowering women and ending male domination.

Peasants*

Farm workers. Some Chinese peasants owned large farms, employed people to work on them, and became wealthy. Others owned little or nothing and were extremely poor.

Censorship*

A government policy that restricts freedom of speech and expression through monitoring newspapers, magazines and other forms of media, and banning articles that are believed to be harmful or critical of the government.

Corruption*

The wrong use of power. Generally, corruption occurs in governments where officials use their power to make themselves wealthy, rather than fulfil their duty.

Inflation*

An economic situation in which there is an ongoing rise in the price of goods and services.

Extend your knowledge

Feminism in China

Feminism emerged in China in the late 19th century. Female intellectuals and journalists used China's newspapers and magazines to discuss women's rights, women's roles and the measures necessary to achieve women's liberation. This debate influenced Mao, Chiang and government policy throughout the 20th century.

CCP strengths

The CCP was in a relatively weak position in 1945, having fewer and more poorly equipped troops than the nationalists, with no aircraft support. It also controlled few cities. However it also had some strengths.

- It controlled much of China's northern countryside.
- It had the support of the peasants, due to the CCP's policy of land reform.
- It had the support of the USSR*.
- The PLA had experience of guerrilla warfare* from fighting the Japanese during the Second World War.

Key terms

USSR*

USSR is short for Union of Soviet Socialist Republics (also shortened to Soviet Union). The republics were Russia, Ukraine, Belarus, Kazakhstan, Turkmenistan and several smaller countries. In theory, all republics were partners in the Union, but in practice it was ruled from Moscow, the capital of Russia.

Guerrilla warfare*

A type of fighting carried out by small bands of fighters, usually civilians, rather than large armies of trained soldiers. Guerrilla tactics include raids, ambushes and hit-and-run attacks.

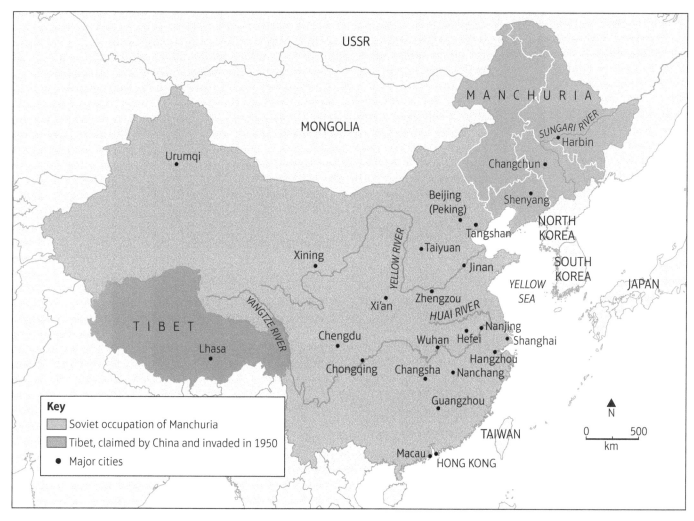

Figure 1.1 A map of China in October 1945.

Timeline

Civil War, 1945–49

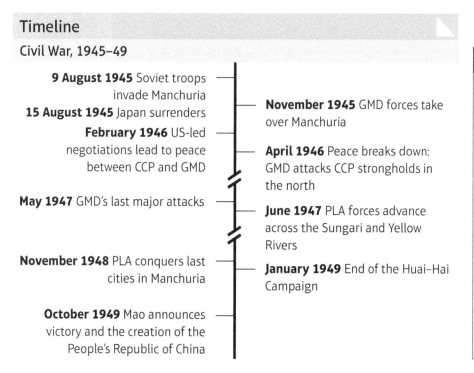

9 August 1945 Soviet troops invade Manchuria

15 August 1945 Japan surrenders

November 1945 GMD forces take over Manchuria

February 1946 US-led negotiations lead to peace between CCP and GMD

April 1946 Peace breaks down: GMD attacks CCP strongholds in the north

May 1947 GMD's last major attacks

June 1947 PLA forces advance across the Sungari and Yellow Rivers

November 1948 PLA conquers last cities in Manchuria

January 1949 End of the Huai–Hai Campaign

October 1949 Mao announces victory and the creation of the People's Republic of China

Activity ?

Design a poster for the CCP to attract support during the Civil War. The poster should:

a set out the CCP's key strengths that are most attractive to China's workers and peasants

b pick out the key problems with the GMD

c use imagery that symbolises the nature of the CCP: search the internet for 'Chinese Civil War posters' for ideas.

You could use a software package to design the poster.

Mao and the events of the Civil War

The Civil War went through a series of phases. Mao Zedong's leadership and approach to the war were key reasons for the CCP's victory by October 1949.

Phase 1: Uneasy peace

At the end of the Second World War there was a brief period of relative peace, with neither side launching major campaigns. From February to April 1946, the US led peace negotiations between the CCP and GMD. However, the peace was unstable because:

- the two sides had very different beliefs
- there was mistrust between the two sides, as a result of years of conflict
- Mao and Chiang both wanted to be sole leader of China.

Therefore, while both sides were involved in peace negotiations, in secret they worked with their allies to strengthen their positions.

Manchuria

In August 1945, the USSR invaded Manchuria in order to defeat the Japanese, who had occupied the region since 1936. The USSR's invasion created problems for the GMD.

- Chiang suspected that the Soviet forces would aid their fellow communists in the CCP.
- Manchuria was in the north-east of China. It bordered the CCP strongholds. Chiang was concerned that the Soviet invasion would lead to the CCP gaining control of the whole of northern China.
- Manchuria contained a great deal of modern industry, as well as large stocks of Japanese weapons. Chiang was concerned that the CCP would get access to these.

To prevent the CCP gaining control of Manchuria, Chiang reached an agreement with the USSR that Soviet forces would control the region until Chiang's forces took control. In November 1945, US military aircraft flew 110,000 GMD troops to Manchuria, giving Chiang control of the region. However, Soviet troops had already allowed the PLA to take 100,000 guns and several thousand pieces of artillery left by the Japanese.

GMD problems in Manchuria

GMD control of Manchuria was not popular.

- Many Manchurian people regarded the GMD as 'southerners', and therefore as foreign invaders.
- The GMD only reopened 852 of Manchuria's 2,411 factories. Consequently, unemployment rose.
- The GMD found it more difficult to control rural areas, where PLA guerrilla units fought GMD forces. By early 1946, the GMD had effectively lost control of Manchuria's rural areas.

Peace negotiations

The USA urged Chiang to establish a united, democratic government*. In February 1946, the GMD and the CCP agreed a ceasefire. However, fighting began again in April. By July, there was full-scale civil war.

> **Key term**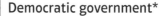
>
> **Democratic government***
> A government that represents the people of a country through competitive elections.

Phase 2: GMD advances

During the ceasefire, both sides strengthened their positions. The CCP extended its control of the northern countryside. At the same time, Chiang persuaded the USA to provide more economic and military support.

From July 1946, the GMD fought to end communist control of territory in the north. By May 1947, the GMD controlled all of the cities across the north of China, except for Harbin.

Mao's role, 1946–47

Mao played a crucial role in the PLA's strategy. He ordered the PLA to retreat. As a result, although the CCP lost control of the cities, the PLA survived. Therefore, the GMD failed to knock Mao's troops out of the war.

Mao also played an important role in consolidating CCP control of the northern countryside. Mao ordered the speeding up of land reform. Peasants were able to take control of the land they worked. As a result, northern peasants began to join the PLA in large numbers.

Source B

A photograph of GMD forces in a US-supplied tank. The photograph was taken in 1947 by an American photographer for *Life*, a popular US magazine which dealt with news and current affairs.

Phase 3: PLA counter-attacks

By mid-1947, unemployment, inflation, corruption and lack of reform meant that the workers of the northern cities had lost faith in GMD rule.

In June, Mao ordered the PLA's first major attacks and was extremely successful. Around 400,000 PLA troops attacked across the Sungari River. The PLA also pushed further south, as Liu Bocheng, one of the PLA's best generals, attacked across the Yellow River.

The PLA's counter-attacks led to a change in the balance of power. The GMD lost control of much of Manchuria and the PLA secured its hold on north-east China.

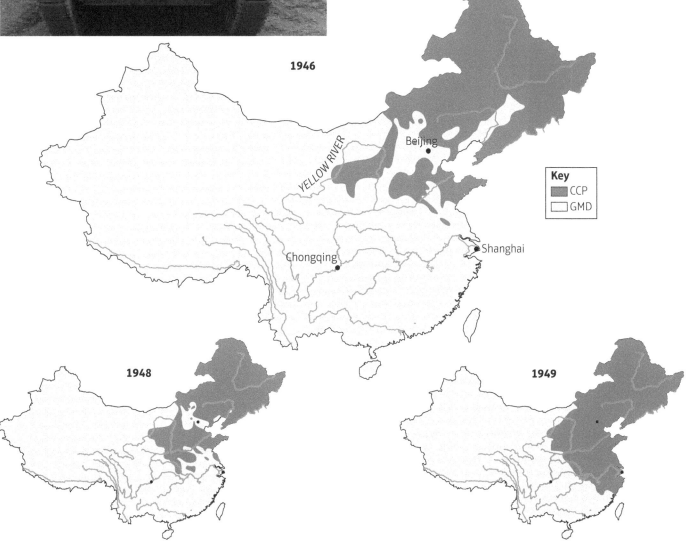

Figure 1.2 Maps of China 1946–49, showing the progress of the CCP in the Civil War.

Mao's role, 1947–48

Mao played a key role during the PLA's first wave of counter-attacks supporting a change in military tactics. During 1946, the PLA had been a guerrilla army. However, from mid-1947, it began to function more like a regular army.

He also backed Liu Bocheng's daring strategy of crossing the Yellow River.

Phase 4: PLA advance

During 1948, the PLA made a series of important advances. The GMD lost its last cities in Manchuria, changing the balance of power and giving a decisive advantage to the CCP. The Huai–Hai Campaign, a victory for the PLA, was the last major battle of the war. From the beginning of 1949, there was little opposition to the PLA's advance south.

Source C

A woodcut by a communist artist, from 1951. It shows the Miao people welcoming the PLA during the Civil War. The Miao live primarily in southern China's mountains.

Activity ?

List the ways in which Source C implies that the PLA were welcomed by the Miao people.

The significance of the loss of Manchuria

Mao had masterminded a highly successful two-part strategy. First, the PLA gained control of the countryside, cutting off the GMD in the cities. Second, the PLA stormed the cities. By November 1948, the PLA had control of the whole of Manchuria.

The GMD's loss of Manchuria was significant for several reasons.

- The GMD had sent large numbers of troops to defend the region. Mao's strategy of surrounding the cities meant that the GMD could not retreat. By the end of 1948, the GMD had lost around one-third of its troops.
- By contrast, CCP control of the north and Manchuria allowed it to recruit more soldiers. By October 1948, 1.6 million peasants had joined the PLA.
- Mao's strategy also allowed the PLA to capture the GMD's weapons. Estimates suggest that, following the loss of Manchuria, the PLA had 22,800 pieces of artillery compared to the GMD's 21,000.
- The loss of Manchuria was a major PLA victory and a big psychological blow for the GMD.

Exam-style question, Section A

Explain why the GMD's loss of Manchuria helped the CCP win the Chinese Civil War.

You may use the following in your answer:
- GMD troop losses
- CCP territorial gains.

You **must** also use information of your own. **12 marks**

Exam tip

When you answer an 'Explain why' question, you need to give reasons that show why something happened. In this case, make sure you don't simply tell the story of the GMD's loss of Manchuria.

The Huai–Hai Campaign

The Huai–Hai Campaign, which lasted from 6 November 1948 until 10 January 1949, was the largest battle and the major turning point of the Civil War. Chiang's army consisted of 800,000 troops. Mao's army was even bigger, comprising 600,000 soldiers, 600,000 guerrilla fighters, and a further 1 million peasants who provided support for the army. In addition, PLA spies infiltrated the GMD and supplied Mao with Chiang's plans. What is more, morale in the GMD was so low that thousands of soldiers switched sides, joining the PLA.

The campaign was named after the location of the battles. Fighting took place between the Huai River and the Huang Hai, or Yellow Sea.

The significance of the Huai–Hai Campaign

The GMD lost 500,000 troops during the campaign: the majority were captured, but 200,000 were killed or injured. The campaign destroyed the GMD's last line of defence and the GMD could do little to stop the PLA's advance over the Yangtze River into the south of China. Following the defeat, Chiang resigned as president of the Republic of China.

Communist victory

During 1949, the PLA moved south, meeting little resistance. The PLA captured the cities of Nanchang and Shanghai in May. Mao proclaimed the creation of the People's Republic of China (PRC) on 1 October 1949. Small-scale fighting continued until April 1950. Chiang and his supporters moved to the island of Taiwan, where Chiang established a new government, becoming president of the Republic of China (ROC) in 1950.

Extend your knowledge

The Founding Ceremony of China

The painting, Source D, was designed to ensure that Mao dominates it. He is placed in the centre, alone, and is slightly taller than the other figures. The painting was subtly changed in the two decades after it was painted. Dong Xiwen, the artist, was required to repaint the group on the left on a number of occasions to remove figures who Mao Zedong had forced out of government. For example, in 1956, Vice President Gao Gang was removed from the painting after he fell out with Mao.

The painting was used widely as a symbol of China's new beginning. It was featured on the cover of the *People's Daily*, China's biggest newspaper, as soon as it was finished, and in school textbooks. The painting was also genuinely popular, and over 1 million copies were sold as posters in the year after it was completed.

Source D

The *Founding Ceremony of China* (1953), an oil painting of Mao Zedong proclaiming the creation of the PRC in October 1949. Behind Mao stand key figures who played an important role in the victory of the CCP, such as Zhou Enlai (second from the left), Lin Biao (third from the left) and Liu Shaoqi (fourth from the left).

Reasons for the CCP's success

The CCP's victory was due to a combination of military skill, tactical brilliance, leadership, popular support and the weaknesses of the GMD. Victory led to the formation of a communist government headed by Mao.

Interpretation 1

From *Communist States in the 20th Century* by Steve Phillips et al., published in 2015.

... civil war between the GMD and CCP broke out in 1946. Although Chiang had overwhelming superiority in resources, he squandered his initial advantage by rushing into a full-scale attack on the Communist strongholds in Manchuria. Having survived the onslaught there, the Communists were gradually able to move south and take over the Nationalist-held areas.

Interpretation 2

From *China at War 1901–1949* by Edward L. Dreyer, published in 2014.

… the communist victory in the Chinese Civil War was attributed, by Chinese as well as foreign analysts, to the specific strategy of the communists. This was sometimes called simply guerrilla warfare, but all of Mao Tse-tung's [Zedong's] military writings note that guerrilla warfare is only part of … [a] 'People's War' … The main elements of People's War … [were] a politically motivated and organised peasantry … [the use of] guerrilla units and … regular forces … [and] 'surrounding the cities from the countryside'.

Exam-style question, Section B

How far do you agree with Interpretation 1 about the reasons for the CCP's victory in the Civil War? Explain your answer, using Interpretations 1 and 2 and your knowledge of the historical context.   **16 marks**

Exam tip

When evaluating an interpretation, do not consider its reliability, as it is not a primary source.

Leadership

Leadership played an important role in the victory of the CCP. Mao ensured that the PLA remained disciplined, and that soldiers treated peasants with respect. Chiang, on the other hand, failed to deal with corruption in the GMD; therefore, people in GMD territories lost faith in their government.

Mao also understood the significance of politics. He supported radical land reform and, in so doing, won over the peasants. Chiang, however, did little to address poverty, unemployment or the continued abuse of women's rights. The GMD failed to win over the Chinese people.

Mao also worked effectively with his top generals, Liu Bocheng and Lin Biao. Chiang's government, by contrast, was divided. For example, Chiang disagreed with Fu Zuoyi, a highly respected general, over strategy.

Interpretation 3

From *The Chinese Civil War 1945-49* by Michael Lynch, published in 2010.

Mao Zedong's record up to 1949 was a truly remarkable one. He had led a vast social revolution, had defeated the Nationalists, and had created the People's Republic of China, the world's largest Communist state. Set against these successes, Chiang Kai-shek's record seemed barren. Having been the dominant force in China … he lost the civil war and was driven from the mainland.

Activities   ?

Read Interpretation 3.

1   Summarise its view in 20 words or less. Having done this, swap your summary with a classmate.

2   Check each other's summaries: if you disagree on the main view of the interpretation, re-read the interpretation together and discuss its meaning.

Military factors

Initially, the GMD had a clear military advantage. Chiang's army was larger than Mao's and had access to US weapons. However, Mao's tactics undercut the GMD's advantage because guerrilla warfare plays to the strengths of small, highly mobile militia* bands.

During the final phases of the war, PLA tactics were superior to those of the GMD. Mao and his generals were able to act decisively and quickly. The GMD, by contrast, tended to be slow and indecisive.

Key term

Militia*

An armed group of ordinary people who are not usually soldiers, but can be called upon to fight when needed.

Economic factors

The GMD's war effort was undermined by the state of the economy. First, the GMD's policies led to inflation. Inflation had important political consequences. Wealthy people who had supported the GMD at the beginning of the Civil War lost faith in the government as their savings lost value.

Unemployment was another economic problem in the GMD zone. GMD leaders tended to sell off industrial machinery and close down factories.

Urban unrest

High unemployment and rising inflation led to industrial unrest. For example, in 1946 there were 1,716 industrial disputes in Shanghai alone. The number of strikes in Shanghai rose to 2,538 in 1947.

The CCP was able to work with groups in the GMD zones in order to organise strikes. For example:

- in 1947, the CCP helped to organise a strike of around 90,000 female textile workers across GMD territory
- telecommunications workers also went on strike, in May 1947.

The GMD fought back, rounding up and executing communists. Nonetheless, strikes disrupted the economy in the GMD zone. The telecommunications strike made it difficult for GMD leaders to co-ordinate their government. Other strikes undermined the GMD's ability to supply its army.

Source E

A photograph of three communists being taken to their execution. The photograph was taken in secret by an American journalist who was reporting from a GMD-controlled region in May 1949.

Source F

This extract is from Derk Bodde's book *Peking Diary*, published in 1950. It describes life in China during the Civil War. Here, the writer describes his experiences in a GMD-controlled city in Manchuria that was being besieged by the CCP. Bodde was an American historian who lived in China during the 1930s and returned to the country in 1948.

Half a million people have left, either for Communist areas or as refugees to North China. Industrial production is down to almost nothing. A primary factor is lack of food, caused by siege. Lack of food results in lowered coal production, which cuts electric power, which in turn leads to flooding of coal mines. Production appears to be coming to a complete standstill. This coming winter there will surely be starvation.

Exam-style question, Section A

Give **two** things you can infer from Source F about the reasons for CCP victory in the Chinese Civil War.

4 marks

Exam tip

You infer something from a source by working out something the source does not actually tell you directly. You should make two inferences when answering this kind of question.

Peasant support

Peasant support was another significant factor in the CCP's victory. Poor peasants gave their food to the PLA and helped transport vital goods, because they associated the GMD with oppressive landlords. During the Huai–Hai Campaign, peasants brought supplies to the PLA in wheelbarrows or on horse-drawn carts.

THINKING HISTORICALLY Interpretations (4a)

The weight of evidence

Historians' interpretations are not simply their opinions – interpretations are theories. In order for theories to be strong, they need to be backed up with convincing evidence. When you evaluate an interpretation, you should consider how strong the evidence is for the conclusions it reaches.

Work in pairs. Read Source F. What does it tell you about the support of people for the CCP? Read the conclusions below, then answer the questions.

Conclusion 1

Many people in China supported the CCP during the Civil War. This is shown by the fact that millions left GMD areas during the war.

Conclusion 2

The people of China supported the CCP during the Civil War. There were economic problems in GMD areas, such as lack of food, so people supported the CCP.

Conclusion 3

Many people left GMD-controlled areas in Manchuria during the Civil War, showing that the CCP was more popular than the GMD in at least some parts of China.

GMD economic policies were not providing enough food or fuel. This explains why support for the GMD was declining.

1 Write out each conclusion and then use highlighter pens to colour-code them. Use one colour for 'evidence', another colour for 'conclusions' and a third for language that shows 'reasoning' (e.g. 'therefore', 'so').

2 How do the conclusions differ in terms of the way that the evidence is used?

3 Put the conclusions in ranking order from the best to the worst. Explain your choice.

4 Consider what you know about support for the CCP and the GMD during the Civil War. For each conclusion, add any extra evidence you can think of that supports that conclusion.

5 Rank the conclusions again. Does the evidence you've added change which you think is the best?

6 Using evidence from the source and your own knowledge, write your own conclusion about the level of support the CCP had during the Civil War. Remember to back up all your points by reasoning about the evidence.

Summary

- In 1946, a full-scale civil war broke out between the CCP and the GMD.
- Mao Zedong, the CCP's leader, played a key role in CCP victory by devising its political and military strategy.
- The CCP became increasingly popular because of the GMD's corruption and failing economic policies.
- The GMD's loss of Manchuria and the CCP's victory in the Huai–Hai Campaign fatally weakened the GMD.

Checkpoint

Strengthen

S1 Describe two key strengths of the CCP during the Civil War.

S2 Give two examples of the problems experienced in the GMD-controlled zone during the Civil War.

S3 Which of the CCP's strengths can be illustrated by its victory in the Huai–Hai Campaign?

Challenge

C1 Summarise two ways in which Mao was responsible for CCP victory.

C2 Explain why the PLA's tactics helped it to win the Civil War.

If you are not confident about any of these questions, form a group with other students, discuss the answers and then record your conclusions. Your teacher can give you some hints.

1.2 Communist rule

Mao Zedong was the dominant figure in the new communist government. His ideology* and his vision of the future shaped the way that the People's Republic of China (PRC) developed.

Mao's ideology

Mao was a Marxist*. He was a creative and innovative thinker whose ideas were also influenced by nationalism, feminism and traditional Chinese philosophy. Mao's ideology is often referred to as Maoism.

Source A

A poster entitled 'Mao the Peasant's Hero', produced by the CCP in 1951. The poster was distributed in rural areas as part of the land reform campaign of the early 1950s.

Nationalism

Mao was influenced by Chinese nationalism. He believed:

- the Chinese people had all the skills and brilliance that they needed to shape their own destiny
- China needed a strong government to fight foreign attempts to enslave the Chinese people.

Key terms

Ideology*

A set of related political ideas. Mao's ideology was made up of ideas about the nature of society, China's role in the world and the best ways in which the government could strengthen the nation.

Marxist*

Follower of an ideology that has its origins in the writings of Karl Marx. Marx was a German writer and philosopher. He argued that society was progressing towards communism – a time when people would be genuinely free and equal. He argued that urban workers had a unique role to play in destroying capitalist society and creating a new communist society.

Women's rights

Mao was also influenced by Chinese feminism. He was committed to:

- ending forced marriage – a practice where young people were required to marry by their families
- banning the sale of women – a practice where men could buy young women as brides.

More generally, Mao believed that women and men should both play a political role.

'Marxism with Chinese characteristics'

The Russian Revolution* of 1917 inspired Mao. The Revolution had led to the creation of a new radical regime. Mao hoped that a similar regime in China would achieve his nationalist goals of creating a strong, united nation.

Chinese society presented problems for Marxists. Marx had argued that communism was only possible in a society with an advanced industrial economy, such as Britain, the USA or Germany. Chinese society was largely rural. Therefore, most Marxists believed that China was not ready for communism.

Nonetheless, Mao believed that it was possible to have a revolution in China. He argued that Marxism could be applied to China, but the result would be a new kind of Marxism that stressed the importance of the peasants. Mao called his new theory 'Marxism with Chinese characteristics'.

Interpretation 1

From *The Politics of China* by Roderick MacFarquhar, published in 1997.

When the People's Republic of China (PRC) was formally established on 1 October 1949 the nation's new leaders faced daunting problems. Society and polity [government] were fragmented, public order and morale had decayed, a war-torn economy suffered from severe inflation and unemployment, and China's fundamental economic and military backwardness created monumental impediments [obstructions] to the elite's goals of national wealth and power.

Activities **?**

Read Interpretation 1.

1 List the problems facing China in 1949.
2 Put the problems into categories in the form of a Venn diagram.
3 Swap diagrams with a classmate. Compare diagrams and see if you used the same categories. If you used different categories, discuss which categories are best suited to this task.

Key term

The Russian Revolution*

A series of events from February 1917 to early 1921 that led to Lenin and the Russian Communist Party establishing a communist government in Russia.

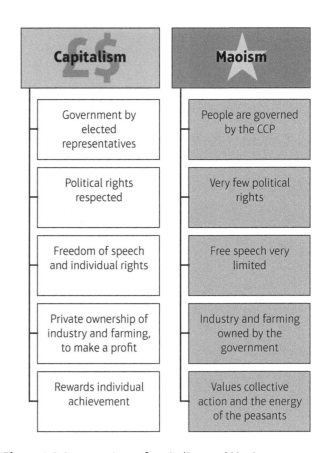

Figure 1.3 A comparison of capitalism and Maoism.

The peasants

Like all Marxists, Mao argued that the proletariat* should play the leading role in a revolution. However, Mao argued that, in China, all people without property would benefit from a revolution. Therefore, he claimed that communists could rely on the peasants to support the revolution. What is more, because peasants made up more than 80% of China's population, Mao argued that the peasants were the key to a successful revolution.

Key term

Proletariat*

A term used by Marxists to refer to the urban working class. Typically, the proletariat work in factories.

The army

Mao argued that the peasants' role was to form a revolutionary army. The army in the countryside should support the CCP in the cities. The army should use guerrilla tactics to surround the cities and liberate them from capitalists* and imperialists*.

Key terms

Capitalists*

For Marxists, a class of people who create wealth by exploiting working people.

Imperialists*

For Marxists, people or nations who want to dominate other nations.

Extend your knowledge

Guerrilla warfare

Mao's ideas about guerrilla warfare were influenced by Chinese military history and Chinese literature. Mao was inspired by Sun Tzu, a Chinese philosopher and military leader who lived around 500 BC. Mao was also inspired by the classic Chinese novels *Outlaws of the Marsh* and the *Romance of the Three Kingdoms*, both of which describe military campaigns conducted by bands of peasants. While Mao was also influenced by Western ideas such as communism, he always respected Chinese literature and philosophy.

The Party

Mao also stressed the importance of the CCP, which he believed had two main roles.

- It should organise the proletariat in China's cities, so that they would be ready to seize power.
- It should lead the peasants. Mao argued that the peasants were incapable of playing a revolutionary role without the guidance of the CCP.

Mao argued that the CCP could play this role because it was a group of dedicated and educated revolutionaries. Workers and peasants lacked the education to create a revolution on their own.

Ideas

Mao's form of Marxism also stressed the importance of ideas. Traditionally, Marxists had emphasised economic factors, such as the growth of industry, as being the most important cause of a revolution. Mao, however, argued that ideas played a key role. He argued that courage and a good understanding of philosophy were just as important.

Source B

A woodcut produced by the CCP in the early 1950s, celebrating the thoughts of Mao Zedong. The picture shows a soldier, an urban worker and a peasant. Each holds a book of Mao's thoughts. The caption reads 'His words bring warmth and life'.

Mao's vision of the future

In 1949, Mao believed that communism was a long way off. Mao believed that the CCP's immediate tasks were to industrialise China, to stamp out opposition, to improve education and to modernise agriculture. In this sense, Mao's initial vision for China was pragmatic* rather than utopian*.

Key terms

Pragmatic*

An approach to politics that is prepared to make changes in order to solve problems.

Utopian*

Utopianism is an approach to politics which tries to create an ideal or perfect world. Utopians focus on political ideals. Utopian politics is often contrasted with pragmatic politics.

The role of Mao

Mao played a central role in the CCP by adapting Marxism to Chinese society. His emphasis on guerrilla warfare gave the CCP a strategy through which it could challenge the GMD. Finally, Mao's emphasis on nationalism was extremely attractive to many who wanted to free China from foreign domination.

Mao's dominant position in the CCP

Mao was the undisputed leader of the CCP. He achieved dominance for a number of reasons.

- He was a successful leader during the Civil War.
- His policy of guerrilla warfare allowed the PLA to survive in the early part of the Civil War, when the GMD had a larger and better equipped army.
- He proved himself as an intellectual* by adapting Marxism to the situation in China.
- He worked successfully with other leading figures in the CCP and the PLA. For example, he worked closely with Lin Biao, a talented general, during the Civil War.
- His ideas were so influential that they became the official basis of the CCP in 1945.

Mao's successful strategies, his history of leading the Party through difficult times and his reputation as an intellectual all helped consolidate his position as Chairman of the CCP.

Key term

Intellectual*

A highly educated person who can learn and reason.

The government of China

Mao described his new government as a 'People's democratic dictatorship'. Initially, it seemed that Mao was committed to democracy. In September 1949, he established the Chinese People's Political Consultative Conference (CPPCC) to create a new constitution. The CPPCC, which included representatives from across China, set out the principles on which the new government should be based. These included freedom of expression, freedom of religion, multi-party elections and equal rights for men and women. The new constitution of 1954 created:

- the National People's Congress (NPC) – a parliament to make China's laws
- Provincial Congresses – a system of local parliaments for the provinces and major cities
- the State Council – elected by the NPC, in charge of all the main government ministries, with Zhou Enlai as the first premier (prime minister) of the State Council
- a president – the head of state and the PLA, elected by the NPC.

Mao was elected as the PRC's first president and chairman of the State Council.

The role of the CCP

In reality, Mao had no intention of working democratically. Indeed, the CCP dominated the government, playing a much larger role than the NPC. Even so, in the early years, the CCP had to work with people from other political parties. In 1949, the CCP did not have enough trained and educated members to fill all of the government's posts. The CCP contained only around 720,000 members who were qualified to work for the government, while there were 2 million government jobs to be done.

Nonetheless, Mao's long-term goal was to replace the former members of the GMD with members of the CCP. The CCP grew in size from 4.5 million in 1949 to 5.8 million in 1950 by encouraging workers to join the Party.

The CCP was a highly centralised* and disciplined political party. Representatives of the CCP met at Regional and National Congresses of the CCP infrequently to make decisions on important issues. The National Congress elected the Central Committee, a group of senior communists who directed the activities of the CCP.

By the end of 1952, the CCP organised all of the important work of the government. It organised the military, the education system, trade unions and the police force. The Politburo, a small committee of the Central Committee of the CCP, became the centre of the Chinese government. Only the Standing Committee of the Politburo, the very top leaders of the CCP, had more power than the Politburo itself. Liu Shaoqi became the first chairman of the Standing Committee.

Key term
Centralised*
A form of organisation in which all government is placed under strong central control.

The role of the PLA

The PLA also played an important role in regional government. China was divided into six vast regions, each controlled by the PLA. The PLA began a campaign to hunt down bandits, killing over 100,000 people believed to be enemies of the CCP between 1950 and 1953.

The PLA also had an important economic role. PLA soldiers rebuilt roads and railways, and were also deployed to construct irrigation systems, to teach in schools and even to breed pigs.

Mao's role within the government

Mao dominated all aspects of government. He was president of the PRC, chairman of the CCP and, as president, head of the PLA. Additionally, Mao effectively chose the Politburo and senior generals. In doing so, he held almost unlimited power.

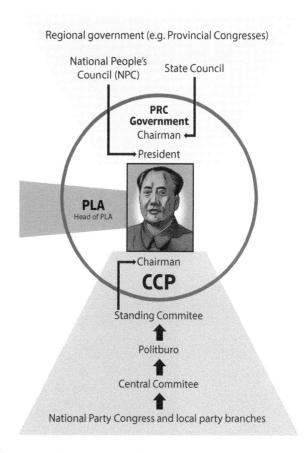

Figure 1.4 The structure of the government of the PRC in 1954, showing Mao's central position as head of all of the major parts of government.

New mass party membership

By 1953, the CCP had a new mass membership of 6.5 million. Mao used the mass membership to:

- consolidate CCP control across China
- introduce land reform across the whole of China
- stop US forces destroying communism in the Korean War (1950–53).

Mao used the same techniques that he had used during the Civil War. Specifically, he used the mass membership to organise mass campaigns, to get the people involved in major projects.

- The CCP organised mass campaigns to suppress their opponents, including the 'antis' movements (see page 29).
- Following the Agrarian Reform Law of 1950, the CCP organised bands of peasants to force landlords to give up their land.

- The Resist America, Aid Korea campaign encouraged workers and peasants to aid the war against capitalism in Korea.

In each case, the CCP organised propaganda* (see Chapter 4) and mass meetings to inspire workers and peasants to give up their free time to implement CCP policy.

Mass party membership was essential to the early phase of the CCP government because the Party was still establishing administrative control across China. Therefore, the CCP had to rely on mass campaigns until it had secured its control.

Source C

A photograph of workers at a clothing factory in Beijing. They are writing a letter to Mao promising to increase the production of military uniforms in order to help the fight against the USA in Korea. The photograph was taken in December 1950 for the official newspaper, the *People's Daily*, shortly after the PRC first sent troops to fight in the Korean War.

Activities ?

Source C shows textile workers writing a collective letter to Mao showing support for the government. In pairs:

1 List reasons that workers and peasants had in 1950 for supporting the CCP.

2 Write a letter to Mao listing reasons why you support the regime. The letter should focus on three main reasons, devoting a paragraph to each.

Key term

Propaganda*

Publications and media designed to promote a persuasive political message.

The Korean War, 1950–53

The Korean War was the first major military conflict of the Cold War*. It began when the communist state of North Korea invaded South Korea, an ally of the USA. The USSR and China backed North Korea.

The Korean War was important for the development of Mao's regime.

- It allowed the government to appeal to Chinese nationalism.
- At mass rallies, the CCP presented the USA as imperialists who were determined to dominate Asia.
- Chinese soldiers were sent to Korea and played a key role in stopping the advance of US troops. This was a major propaganda victory for Mao as he could claim his forces had stopped the army of a superpower*.
- The government spread a rumour that US forces were using biological weapons against communist soldiers, which created outrage in China.
- The CCP argued that there were American spies in the government, and therefore purged and executed as many as 135,000 people in the first six months of the war alone.

For many in China, stopping US forces in the Korean War undid a century of Chinese humiliation and re-established China as a world power.

Key terms

Cold War*

A period of military competition and high tension between the USSR and the USA, without direct military conflict between them.

Superpower*

One of the world's two major powers (the USSR and USA), which had a combination of significant economic and military power.

Source D

From *The Private Life of Chairman Mao* by Zhisui Li, published in 1996. Zhisui Li was Mao's personal doctor for more than 20 years. He remembers the impact of the Korean War on China.

I followed the war closely, surprised and thrilled that China was not only holding its own but was actually defeating the United States forces in battle after battle. It was the first time in more than a century that China was engaged in war with a foreign power without losing face. I was appalled, too, over reports that the United States was using bacteriological [biological] warfare in Korea. Even as the Korean War dragged on ... I was proud to be Chinese.

Activities ?

Read Source D.

1 List the reasons why the author feels proud of China.

2 Write a sentence explaining what you can infer from Source D about the impact of the Korean War on the popularity of Mao's government.

Interpretation 2

From *The People's Republic of China 1949–76* by Michael Lynch, published in 2010.

[The Korean War] did have some positive results for Communist China: The government's call for national unity ... helped ... the CCP to consolidate their hold over China ... The 3-year experience of war hardened China's resolve to stand alone in a hostile world. The PRC could justifiably claim that for 3 years it had matched the USA in combat and remained undefeated.

Interpretation 3

From *Communist States in the Twentieth Century* by Andrew Flint, published in 2015.

Mao was able to use the [Korean] war ... to purge his enemies on the pretence of them being spies or traitors. Collective spirit was forged in mass meetings that whipped up hatred for the USA. The 'Resist America, Aid Korea' campaign denounced the Americans as 'bandits, murderers and savages'. ... The regime spread a rumour that the Americans were testing biological weapons.

Activities ?

Read Source D and Interpretations 2 and 3.

1 Divide a large sheet of paper in two. On one side, list the claims made in Source D about how the Korean War made the author feel about China. On the other side, list the claims made by Interpretations 2 and 3 about the benefits of the Korean War for the CCP and the PRC.

2 Write a sentence evaluating how far Source D supports the view of Interpretations 2 and 3.

Source E

Chinese students volunteering to join the PLA in order to defend North Korea. The photograph was taken in Beijing in December 1950 by a Chinese press photographer.

Democratic centralism

The CCP was organised according to the principle of democratic centralism.

- All Party members could participate in debates about the future of China.
- All Party members could vote on key issues or send delegates to the National Party Congress.
- Once a policy was agreed, discussion stopped and all members had a duty to help implement the policy.

Democratic centralism played a role in managing members. Loyal members who implemented policy without question were promoted, whereas disloyal members who spoke out against policies could be demoted or expelled from the Party. This system of patronage* helped the leaders of the CCP retain control over its members.

In practice, China's government was not very centralised in the first five years of communist rule. From 1949 to 1954, the CCP lacked the expertise or the infrastructure* to control the whole of China. Therefore, a great deal was left to the PLA and the regional branches of the CCP.

Key terms

Patronage*

A form of power based on the ability to promote the careers of others.

Infrastructure*

The structure of roads, railways, canals and communication links that help a modern government control a country. Infrastructure is also crucial to running a modern economy.

Summary

- Mao was the leading figure in the CCP because of his ideas and the success of his strategies.
- Mao held all of the key roles in the government of the PRC from 1949.
- Mao used the PLA and the growing CCP to control China in the years following the creation of the PRC.

Checkpoint

Strengthen

S1 Describe two campaigns that the CCP used to extend its power in the years 1949–51.

S2 List Mao's titles within the Chinese government in 1949.

S3 Summarise Mao's role in the government of the CCP in the years 1949–50.

Challenge

C1 Explain why mass campaigns helped the CCP to consolidate power in the years 1949–50.

C2 Explain the role played by the CCP and the PLA in the government of China in the years 1949–50.

If you are not sure about any of these questions, discuss the possible answers in pairs and then record your conclusions. Your teacher can give you some hints.

1.3 Consolidating the CCP's hold on power, 1951–52

From 1951–52, Mao used terror to intimidate or kill his opponents. This development had a number of causes.

- As the CCP grew in strength, it moved against people it considered to be enemies of the regime.
- The outbreak of the Korean War in 1950 led to concerns that the US would invade China. Mao felt that the CCP government was vulnerable. Therefore, he unleashed terror in order to stop the CCP's enemies from seizing the opportunity of starting a counter-revolution*.
- Mao wanted to strengthen CCP control in the territories it had won in the last years of the Civil War. He used terror to eliminate supporters of the GMD in the south.
- Resistance to land reform had led to the deaths of 3,000 CCP officials in 1950. As a result, Mao ordered the use of terror to help redistribute land to the peasants.

Key term

Counter-revolution*

An attempt to overthrow a revolutionary government. Usually, counter-revolutions try to re-establish the government that had existed before the revolution.

Extend your knowledge

Policy development

Between 1949 and 1957, the CCP tested its key policies in the north-east of China, before introducing them across the rest of the country. For example, the CCP's land reform and the 'antis' movements were first tried out in Manchuria. This was because Manchuria was an area in which CCP control was secure.

The use of terror

Mao authorised the wave of terror in February 1951, in a decree entitled *'Regulations Regarding the Punishment of Counter Revolutionaries'*. The decree gave the CCP's security services authority to persecute a wide range of potential enemies in the cities and the countryside, including religious leaders, who were an alternative source of authority to the CCP. After the Civil War, the CCP had given everybody a class label that specified their family background, social status and occupation. 'Good' classes included revolutionary soldiers, poor peasants and industrial workers; 'bad' classes included landlords, capitalists, rich peasants and 'bad elements' (criminals). Soon these labels were simplified into 'black' or 'red' categories, enemies or friends of the revolution. Those in black categories became the targets of CCP campaigns against counter-revolutionaries.

Source A

A propaganda poster with the message 'Suppress counter-revolutionaries, safeguard good circumstances!' It was produced by the CCP in 1951.

鎮壓反革命,保障好光景！

Urban terror

In the cities, terror focused on intellectuals, property owners and government officials who had worked with the GMD. The terror was designed to be very public. Large meetings were held, at which people were publicly accused of being counter-revolutionaries. The accused were expected to make humiliating public confessions. Many were sentenced to death. The CCP encouraged urban workers to hunt down former members of the GMD and bring them to mass meetings. The mass meetings were often broadcast on radio. Newspapers published lists of people who had committed political crimes.

The terror was public because it was designed to ensure that people were too scared to rebel. The atmosphere of fear in the cities was so intense that hundreds of thousands of people committed suicide.

Estimates suggest that around 2% of the urban population was targeted during 1951. However, in areas which had been GMD strongholds, the percentage was higher: thousands were executed and even more humiliated.

Rural terror

In the countryside, the terror was different. The PLA and the CCP used the terror to speed up the process of land reform and to attack local religious leaders.

- Members of the PLA and the CCP used terror against landlords who refused to surrender their land.
- Land reform committees, which had been set up in 1950, were 'purified'. Wealthier peasants were expelled from the committees and poor peasants were put in charge.
- PLA teams encouraged whole villages to turn against their landlords. As a result, landlords were evicted from their properties, beaten, expelled from villages and, in many cases, killed.
- Landlords were put on trial by local people. Mass meetings were organised in which peasants were encouraged to 'speak bitterness' against the landlords, reminding them of their crimes.
- Landlords were fined for their crimes and had their land, houses and possessions confiscated.

As a result of the rural terror, around 1 million landlords were killed and around 40% of China's land was redistributed to poor peasants. The terror proved popular with the poorest peasants, who made up 70% of the population, as it allowed them to take land and resulted in them paying less taxes.

Source B

From William Hinton's book, *Fanshen: A Documentary of Revolution in a Chinese Village*. Hinton was an American Marxist who travelled to China to study the revolution. The passage describes the redistribution of property which took place in a village in western China in early 1950.

Other makeshift tables, closer still to the temple steps, were laden with clothes of all shapes, sizes, colours, and styles ... Here also were ... silver bracelets, some earrings and other jewellery ornaments ... [and] two alarm clocks ... Another table was piled high with cotton and silk quilts. Here on display was the whole ... wealth of several prosperous ... families, all of which had been transformed by bitter struggle into 'fruits' belonging to the people.

Every item had been carefully recorded by a committee of poor peasants ...

Activity ?

Study Source B. Write a sentence explaining what you can infer from Source B about the reasons why China's peasants supported Mao's government in 1950.

Source C

From an account by Deng Xiaoping published in 2005 by Luo Pinghan. He is describing the rural terror in Western Anhui in the early 1950s. Deng was mayor of Chongqing at the time of the land reform and was responsible for leading it in Anhui.

The masses would hate a few landlords and want them killed, so according to the wishes of the masses we would have these landlords killed. Afterwards the masses would fear reprisals from those who had ties to those we had just killed, and would draw up an even bigger list of names, saying if these people were also killed, everything would be alright ... We kept on killing, and the masses felt more and more insecure.

THINKING HISTORICALLY ▸ **Evidence (4a&b)**

The 'weight' of evidence

One useful idea to have in mind when interpreting historical sources is 'consistency' (whether or not sources support each other). If a number of sources appear to suggest the same conclusion about the past, then we might feel more confident about accepting this conclusion.

However, we should also consider the nature of the sources and the reasons why sources might seem to disagree.

Sources B and C could be used by the historian to build up a picture of how violent land reform was in China, 1949–53.

1 Explain how Sources B and C differ in their views of the violence of land reform.

2 How can the different views taken by the sources be explained? Why do they say different things? Write down as many reasons as you can.

Discuss the following in groups:

3 Suppose the historian had ten more accounts that agreed broadly with Source B and only four that agreed with Source C. Would this mean that Source B was nearer to the truth? Explain your answer.

4 What else should we consider, apart from 'the balance of the evidence', when drawing conclusions from sources such as these?

The 'antis' movements

The urban and rural terror of 1951 helped to consolidate the position of the CCP. However, Mao wanted to go further and therefore launched two new mass campaigns. These 'antis' movements extended the terror, targeting specific groups that Mao believed posed a threat to CCP power.

The 'three antis' movement

In December 1951, Mao launched *Sanfan*: the 'three antis' movement. It was designed to challenge three problems within the government:

- waste
- corruption
- inefficiency.

In reality, the movement targeted officials, based in the cities, who had worked with the previous government. Mao was suspicious of the bureaucracy* and wanted it reformed. The campaign focused specifically on officials who were responsible for managing the economy.

The consequences of the 'three antis' movement

The 'three antis' movement led to a wave of terror. As in the earlier terror, urban workers were encouraged to take part in the campaign. Once again, officials were publicly humiliated before being sacked from their government posts. People who refused to confess were tortured. Around 4 million people were investigated; just over a quarter of them were convicted: they were sent to prison or labour camps or executed.

Extend your knowledge

Mao and bureaucracy

Mao was very critical of bureaucracy and bureaucrats. He was concerned that many members of the CCP who became bureaucrats stopped being true revolutionaries dedicated to the welfare of the workers and peasants, and started looking after their own interests instead.

Key term

Bureaucracy*

Administration, essential to all major organisations.

The people who were arrested worked in government administration. Therefore, the 'three antis' movement stopped the government working effectively. For example, in some regions, the government no longer had the personnel necessary to collect tax. The CCP was also targeted: around 200,000 members were arrested, which disrupted the working of the Party.

The main consequence of the campaign was to expel people from the government that Mao did not trust, and therefore to ensure greater CCP control. The campaign caused huge disruption in the government, so Mao was forced to end it after only a month.

The 'five antis' movement

The 'five antis' movement, known as *Wufan*, was launched in January 1952. Again, Mao used a mass movement of urban workers to attack his enemies. The 'five antis' focused on five key problems in industry:

- bribery
- tax evasion
- fraud
- theft of government property
- theft of government secrets.

Source D

A woodcut created by a CCP artist showing the public humiliation of a 'slacker', a lazy person. The picture was printed in 1951 around the time of the 'three antis' movement.

The real target of the campaign were the people who ran industry, the national bourgeoisie*. In this sense, the 'five antis' movement was an attack on China's capitalists. Teams of CCP members would raid and investigate businesses until they believed they found evidence of a crime. Urban workers and trade unions were encouraged to put capitalists on trial.

Key term

National bourgeoisie*

Chinese capitalists who worked with the communists against the Japanese during the Second World War.

The consequences of the 'five antis' movement

As in previous campaigns, people who were accused of crimes were expected to confess in public. The bosses of 450,000 companies were put on trial meaning the movement affected almost every major business in China. Only around 1% of those put on trial went to prison or labour camps; the rest paid heavy fines.

The main result of the 'five antis' movement was an increase in government control over the economy. The campaign frightened business owners into collaborating with the government. What is more, the large fines gave the government much more money to invest in industry. Finally, the vast majority of major businesses had to pay such large fines that they went bankrupt. Therefore, the government took over the bankrupt firms, extending government control over many businesses. In this sense, the 'five antis' campaign laid an important foundation for the first Five-Year Plan (see page 60), Mao's first attempt to industrialise the economy.

Together, the two 'antis' campaigns resulted in widespread humiliation and suffering. For example, it is estimated that around 200,000 people committed suicide as a result of these campaigns alone.

Activities ?

1. Draw a timeline of the period 1949–53. Include the two 'antis' movements, the Korean War and the terror.
2. Write a paragraph explaining in what ways Mao consolidated his power in the period 1949–52.

Interpretation 1

From *The Politics of China* by Roderick MacFarquhar, published in 1997.

[The] Three Antis Campaign against corrupt cadres [officials], [and] the Five Antis drive against the hitherto respected national bourgeoisie … were extremely intense and generated considerable tension and apprehension in society. … official violence was used on a substantial scale … In addition, intense psychological pressure was brought to bear by various measures, including forced confessions and mass trials … This not only fostered a climate of distrust … it also resulted in large numbers of suicides – possibly … several hundred thousand.

Interpretation 2

From *Mao's China and After: A History of the People's Republic* by Maurice Meisner, published in 1999.

Sanfan fell hardest on the bureaucracy, especially old Guomindang officials … Less than 5 per cent of administrative functionaries were subjected to formal punishment; some were imprisoned, but most were simply dismissed or demoted.

The *Wufan* campaign was a movement of greater … significance. Directed against corrupt practices in the urban economy … its main weight fell on the bourgeoisie …

The new regime was … repressive, but the cities were governed honestly and efficiently for the first time in modern Chinese history.

Exam-style question, Section B

Study Interpretations 1 and 2. They give different views about the impact of the 'antis' movements on China in the early 1950s. What is the main difference between these views? Explain your answer, using details from both interpretations. **4 marks**

Exam tip

The key thing is to focus on the main difference between the interpretations, rather than differences of detail. In this case, focus on what Interpretation 1 and Interpretation 2 argue about the impact of the 'antis' movements.

Summary

- In 1949–50 the CCP collaborated with business owners and former members of the GMD to govern China.
- In 1951–52 the terror and the 'antis' movements extended CCP control over the government and the economy.

Checkpoint

Strengthen

S1 Describe two ways in which the 'antis' movements terrorised Mao's victims.

S2 Describe two consequences of the 'five antis' movement.

S3 Describe the key stages by which the CCP consolidated its power in the years 1949–52.

Challenge

C1 Summarise the causes of the 'antis' campaigns.

C2 How far had the CCP consolidated its power over China by the end of 1952?

If you are not confident about answering these questions, write a list of all factors related to the issues. Then use your notes on this chapter to help you.

Learning outcomes

- Understand Mao's reasons for encouraging criticism of the CCP.
- Understand the events and consequences of the Hundred Flowers campaign.
- Understand Mao's change of policy and the significance of the 'Anti-Rightist' purge.

The Hundred Flowers campaign of 1956–57 was a period of greater freedom in which Mao encouraged scientists, writers and artists to criticise the regime. Mao initiated the campaign in 1956 and encouraged its growth in 1957 but, by the middle of 1957, it was clear that the period of free speech was over.

Mao's reasons for the Hundred Flowers campaign

The Hundred Flowers campaign had several causes. Some were due to events within China; some reflected what was happening in Europe.

Domestic causes

Mao played a leading role in initiating the Hundred Flowers campaign. He was concerned that the CCP needed to be reformed. He was worried that the CCP was:

- getting out of touch with workers and peasants
- becoming a privileged elite who were more interested in their own power than in serving the people
- inefficient and therefore an obstacle to further economic development.

Mao was concerned that there had been a series of industrial strikes during 1956, demanding better pay. He worried that CCP officials were not behaving properly. Therefore, he launched the campaign so that people could speak out against corrupt and inefficient CCP officials and experts.

At the same time, Mao believed that the people genuinely supported CCP rule, due to the success of CCP economic policies. He believed they would use freedom of expression to praise the CCP.

Source A

A popular demonstration in Beijing in favour of communist rule. The photograph was taken by a Chinese press photographer in 1955.

Interpretation 1

From *The Politics of China* by Roderick MacFarquhar, published in 1997.

[By] 1957 the leaders of the Chinese Communist Party (CCP) could look back on the period since 1949 with considerable satisfaction. A strong centralised state had been established, China's national pride and international prestige had grown significantly as a result of fighting the world's greatest power to a stalemate in Korea, the country had taken major steps on the road to industrialisation and achieved an impressive rate of economic growth, and the nation's social system had been transformed according to Marxist precepts in relatively smooth fashion.

> **Activity** ?
>
> Imagine you are Mao's speech writer. Based on Interpretation 1 and your own knowledge of the period 1949–57, write a speech explaining why the CCP has decided to launch the Hundred Flowers campaign. The speech should give at least three reasons and should start with the most important reason.

Finally, the Chinese economy was entering a new phase in the mid-1950s. The economy had recovered from the destruction of the Civil War, and the CCP was planning to build new factories, power stations, bridges and canals. To achieve this, the CCP needed the support of highly educated experts, technicians and intellectuals. Mao hoped that allowing greater freedom of speech – a period of 'blooming and contending' – would persuade Chinese intellectuals to support the regime and to help with the task of economic development.

Source B

From Mao's speech to the Supreme State Conference. The speech was given on 27 February 1957.

Letting a hundred flowers blossom and a hundred schools of thought contend is the policy for promoting the progress of the arts and sciences and a flourishing socialist culture ... Different ... styles in art should develop freely ... We think that it is harmful to the growth of art and science ... to impose one particular style or school of thought and to ban another. ...

In 1956, small numbers of workers or students ... went on strike. ... But a more important cause was bureaucracy on the part of ... [the] leadership. ...

But when disturbances do occur, they enable us to learn lessons, to overcome bureaucracy ...

International causes

The Hundred Flowers campaign was also a response to events in Europe. In 1953, Joseph Stalin, the Soviet dictator, died. His death led to a period of liberalisation in the USSR and in the Eastern bloc*. In February 1956, the Soviet leader Nikita Khrushchev gave a secret speech criticising Stalin and demanding reform. Mao believed that China should play a leading role in this new phase of communism by allowing greater freedom of speech.

Secondly, there had been unrest in the communist states of Hungary and Poland in response to Khrushchev's speech. In both countries the governing communist party almost lost power. Mao believed that communist parties in Europe had lost touch with the people and become corrupt. Mao launched the Hundred Flowers campaign to ensure that the CCP did not become as out of touch as the Polish and Hungarian communist parties.

> **Key term**
>
> **Eastern bloc***
> Communist countries in the east of Europe, for example East Germany, Poland and Hungary, essentially controlled by the USSR.

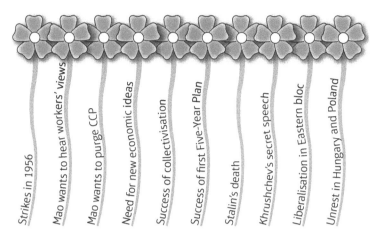

Figure 1.5 The causes of the Hundred Flowers campaign.

Labels on stems: Strikes in 1956 · Mao wants to hear workers' views · Mao wants to purge CCP · Need for new economic ideas · Success of collectivisation · Success of first Five-Year Plan · Stalin's death · Khrushchev's secret speech · Liberalisation in Eastern bloc · Unrest in Hungary and Poland

Mao speaks out

On 27 February 1957, Mao repeated a speech he had given in 1956, called *'On the correct handling of contradictions among the people'*. The speech invited intellectuals to criticise certain aspects of the CCP, such as their approach to art, science, technology and the way in which the CCP administered China. However, Mao warned that intellectuals should not criticise political issues. He stated that he believed that experts should be free to express constructive criticism, and therefore that they could express their views in China's newspapers and magazines. Initially, intellectuals had stayed quiet. They feared that Mao's speech was a trap, designed to catch people who did not support the regime. However, after assurances from the government, intellectuals and experts began to make use of the freedom that Mao had promised.

Interpretation 2

From *A History of China* by Morris Rossabi, published in 2013.

In February [1956], the Soviet leader, Nikita Khrushchev (1894–1971), startled the communist world, particularly the Chinese, with a secret speech … condemning the crimes of the Stalin era. …

Mao responded with a speech in 1956 (published in February of 1957) directed mostly at intellectuals, who could be disruptive but also had skills required for Chinese development. He urged them to make public their complaints and their critiques [criticisms] of the Communist Party and the government. Such dialogues and conversations would permit 'one hundred flowers' to bloom.

Interpretation 3

From *The People's Republic of China 1949–76* by Michael Lynch, published in 2010.

Mao travelled extensively in China during the early 1950s. The rapturous reception he received wherever he went convinced him that he was in touch with the people. In 1956 he informed his government and party colleagues that it would now be an appropriate time to allow greater freedom of expression to those who might wish to comment constructively on how well Communist China was achieving its aim of turning the nation into a proletarian state.

Early in 1957 Mao urged Communist Party officials to be prepared to undergo criticism from the people. With the slogan, 'Let a hundred flowers bloom, let a hundred schools of thought contend', he called on critics within the party to state openly where they thought the government and the CCP had gone wrong.

Activities ?

Read Interpretations 2 and 3.

1 Summarise the view in Interpretation 2 of the causes of the Hundred Flowers campaign. Do the same for Interpretation 3.

2 Write a paragraph explaining which view you agree with most.

3 Swap paragraphs with a classmate and compare them. Discuss which is most persuasive, and why.

Exam-style question, Section B

How useful are Sources C and D for an enquiry into the reasons why Mao launched the Hundred Flowers campaign? Explain your answer, using Sources C and D and your knowledge of the historical context.

8 marks

Exam tip

Source questions like this require you to evaluate the usefulness of two sources. But you do not have to make a judgement about which source is more useful.

Source C

From the memoir of Zhisui Li, Mao's doctor and personal friend. The memoir was published in 1995, after Mao's death and after Zhisui had emigrated to the USA.

Mao's policy of ... 'letting one hundred flowers bloom' ... was a gamble ... based on ... [Mao's belief] that genuine counterrevolutionaries were few ... Mao had reason to believe that his gamble would work. Every time he met with representatives of the 'democratic parties', he was showered with ... flattery ... In the end, Mao's own leadership was criticised. ... Mao of course was shocked. He had never intended that any of the criticisms be directed against him. ... Certain that his real enemies had been eliminated or put in jail, he had not realised the depth of the intellectuals' dissatisfaction.

Source D

From an article by Mao Zedong published in the *People's Daily* on 1 July 1957.

The purpose [of our recent Hundred Flowers campaign] was to let demons and devils, ghosts and monsters 'air views freely' and let poisonous weeds sprout and grow ... so that the people would take action to wipe them out. In other words, the Communist Party foresaw this inevitable class struggle between the bourgeoisie and the proletariat.

For we made it plain to the enemy beforehand: only when ghosts and monsters are allowed to come into the open can they be wiped out; only when poisonous weeds are allowed to sprout from the soil can they be uprooted.

Key features of the campaign

The Hundred Flowers campaign went through a series of phases. First, in December 1956, experts began to express limited criticisms of the regime. For example: scientists and technicians criticised CCP interference in the development of new factories and new technologies and economists criticised CCP interference in the running of the economy. Mao welcomed these criticisms, and his response encouraged more radical criticisms.

The second phase of the campaign began in January 1957, when radical writers joined the campaign. For example, Liu Pin-yan, a writer and journalist, published

a story about lazy and corrupt PLA officials who stood in the way of talented engineers who wanted to build a bridge. This new wave of criticism against the way the CCP governed was unpopular within the CCP. However, once again, Mao supported the criticism.

Chinese students led the final phase of the campaign, which lasted from March to June 1957. Starting at Beijing University, students began criticising key aspects of communist rule. For example, they demanded free speech and free elections. Students began publishing their own magazines and newspapers, over which the CCP had no control. Some even began criticising Mao's use of terror and demanding an end to CCP rule.

Activity ?

Read Source E. Write a newspaper article covering Mao's meeting with the students. The article should:

a explain the context of the meeting

b define what Mao means by 'construction'

c explain at least two ways in which Mao tries to persuade students to support the regime

d explain what can be inferred from the source about the criticisms of CCP rule made by students.

The article should be no more than 150 words long and should contain direct quotes from the source.

Source E

From a conversation between Mao and representatives of the All-China Federation of Students. The conversation took place in the context of student protests in favour of greater freedom. Mao was speaking on 14 February 1957 in Beijing.

Only beginning in 1949 was land reform carried out throughout the country ... You see, revolution is such [a] prolonged [process]; we have only engaged in construction for a few years: how can there be no difficulties? There are over 600 million people in our entire country. It is unlikely that we won't encounter any difficulties ... Construction is even more difficult than revolution.

... The difficulties belong to the young people. The young must succeed the older generation. This is why you must be well-prepared. In the future, the country will be managed by you.

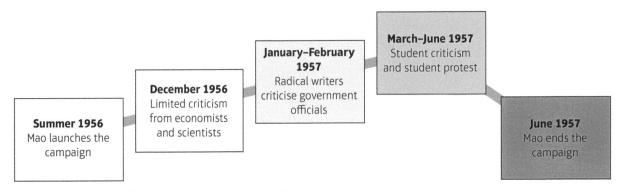

Figure 1.6 The main stages of the Hundred Flowers campaign.

Mao's reaction to the campaign

From the beginning of the campaign until April 1957, Mao supported criticism of the regime. However, from the beginning of 1957, Mao was under increasing pressure to end the campaign. Senior members of the CCP found student protests particularly disturbing because the students had benefited greatly from communist rule, through their university education. Yet, rather than being grateful, they were the harshest critics of the regime. Mao was also concerned about the criticisms made by students. Until February, Mao and the CCP had remained in control of the campaign. However, by publishing their own magazines and starting to criticise key features of CCP government, the students had taken control of the campaign. As a result, in June 1957, Mao ended the campaign, rejecting 'poisonous weeds' (see Source D), and began to clamp down on opposition.

The 'Anti-Rightist' purge

Mao's response to the growing criticism was to purge his opponents. The 'Anti-Rightist'* purge was similar to the earlier 'antis' movements, as the CCP's critics were publicly humiliated and forced to make apologies.

Key features of the 'Anti-Rightist' purge

The 'Anti-Rightist' purge had a number of key features.

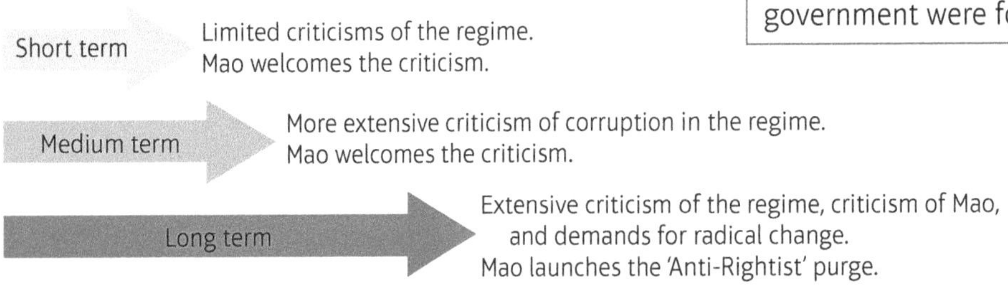

- It attacked many of the intellectuals and students whom Mao had encouraged to speak out during the Hundred Flowers campaign. Between 300,000 and 500,000 people were sent to *Laogai* camps*.

- The campaign emphasised the ideological education of workers and peasants. The CCP used the campaign to challenge the criticisms of it by setting up educational programmes for workers and peasants, to teach them about the benefits of CCP rule.

- Mao acknowledged that there were problems in the CCP and the government. Therefore, he tightened his control over the Party to deal with 'bureaucratic elements' who he felt were undermining faith in the Party. Mao ordered a purge of the Party. Between 5% and 10% of top officials were demoted, sacked or sent to *Laogai* camps to be 're-educated'.

> ### Key terms
>
> **Rightist***
>
> Politics is often described in terms of Left and Right. In China, Mao used 'Rightist' as a term to describe people and groups who wanted to end CCP rule and restore capitalism. The term implied that the CCP was on the Left.
>
> ***Laogai* camps***
>
> Prison labour camps where opponents of the government were forced to work.

Short term — Limited criticisms of the regime. Mao welcomes the criticism.

Medium term — More extensive criticism of corruption in the regime. Mao welcomes the criticism.

Long term — Extensive criticism of the regime, criticism of Mao, and demands for radical change. Mao launches the 'Anti-Rightist' purge.

Figure 1.7 The consequences of the Hundred Flowers campaign.

The consequences of the purge

The 'Anti-Rightist' purge strengthened Mao's position in the CCP. First, many believed that Mao had introduced the Hundred Flowers campaign as a trap to encourage enemies of the CCP to reveal themselves. Many in the CCP felt that this was a clever tactic and proved that Mao was still in control of events.

Second, Mao used criticisms of the CCP to strengthen his control over the Party. This included purging the membership. But Mao also used the opportunity to force the government's premier and foreign minister, Zhou Enlai, to make a public apology for failing to implement Mao's economic policies quickly enough. Zhou's apology was significant because he was one of the most senior figures in the Party. Zhou was China's premier from 1949 until his death in 1976 and also foreign minister from 1949 to 1958, and one of Mao's key supporters. Essentially, Mao used him as a scapegoat, blaming him for the problems in CCP policy. His apology and public humiliation indicated that no one in the CCP was safe from the campaign.

Third, in the long run, experts and intellectuals were fearful of criticising the Party. This meant that experts no longer challenged CCP economic policies. As a result, CCP policies no longer benefited from the insight of experts, which led to economic problems in the later 1950s and early 1960s.

The 'Anti-Rightist' purge ended the brief period of freedom of expression. Mao used the campaign to deal with his enemies outside the CCP and to strengthen his control over the CCP.

Activities ?

Read Interpretations 4 and 5.

1 Working in pairs, summarise the main argument of each interpretation in a single sentence.
2 Organise a debate, with one group arguing that Mao deliberately planned to use the Hundred Flowers campaign as a trap, and another group arguing that Mao was forced to end the campaign because he lost control of the movement.
3 At the end of the debate, vote on which of the two perspectives is most convincing.

Interpretation 4

From *Mao Zedong's China* by Kathlyn Gay, published in 2012.

[Some historians] argue that Mao deliberately planned to weed out enemies … – 'coax the snakes out of their holes,' as he told his personal physician Li Zhisui. …

… Those who had spoken out were labelled 'rightists', and an Anti-Rightist Campaign began in mid-May 1957. Thousands of rightists were sent to prison or labour camps or were executed. … The campaign effectively silenced most Chinese.

Interpretation 5

From *Politics and Purges in China* by Frederick C. Teiwes, published in 1993.

After four to five weeks of … unchecked criticism, the Anti-Rightist Campaign was launched … This action followed about three weeks of reassessing the situation at the highest levels [of the CCP]. … it was clearly a direct response to growing student unrest … A number of events then occurred on May 25 further signalling a shift in policy. Most significant was a statement by Mao to … the Youth League Congress that 'all words and actions that deviate from the cause of socialism are wrong.'

Exam-style question, Section B

Suggest **one** reason why Interpretations 4 and 5 give different views about Mao's reasons for launching the 'Anti-Rightist' purge. You may use Sources C and D to help explain your answer. **4 marks**

Exam tip

When explaining the differences between interpretations, you could point out that different historians use different pieces of evidence. Indeed, Interpretations 4 and 5 indicate that the evidence from the time can lead to different views about Mao's reasons for launching the 'Anti-Rightist' purge.

> ## THINKING HISTORICALLY Interpretations (2a)
>
> ### The importance of selection
>
> Historians do not aim to tell us about the whole past – there is just too much of it. They need to choose which aspects of the past to investigate and which details are most important to examine. For example, an overview history of military strategy during the First World War would be unlikely to examine witness statements about conditions in the trenches in detail, whereas a work about the experience of the ordinary soldier might examine such witness statements in great depth.
>
> ### The role of Mao – some key information
>
> A) He played a key role in PLA strategy during the Civil War.
>
> B) He ordered land reform in CCP areas during the Civil War.
>
> C) He was the dominant figure in the communist government of China.
>
> D) He was a Marxist.
>
> E) He used terror to intimidate or kill his opponents.
>
> F) He initiated the Hundred Flowers campaign.
>
> G) He was chairman of the CCP.
>
> H) He worked well with his generals during the Civil War.
>
> I) He believed the peasants should play a key role in the revolution.
>
> J) He used guerrilla tactics during the Civil War.
>
> K) He was president of the PRC.
>
> L) He ended the Hundred Flowers campaign when he lost control of it.
>
> **1** Often, historians have to focus on a particular question to investigate. What information from points A–L would you use to write about the topics below (you can choose up to four pieces of information)?
>
> a) Mao's role in Chinese government.
>
> b) Mao's ideology.
>
> c) The methods Mao used to rule China.
>
> d) Mao's significance during the Civil War.
>
> With a partner, discuss the following questions and write down your conclusions:
>
> **2** Why is it important to be selective about the information that you put in your historical writing?
>
> **3** How important are the questions that historians ask, in deciding what information is included in their writing?

Summary

- Stalin's death, events in Europe and Mao's belief that the CCP was secure led him to launch the Hundred Flowers campaign.
- The campaign led to growing criticism of the CCP and of Mao himself.
- Mao ended the campaign and punished his critics through the 'Anti-Rightist' purge.

Checkpoint

Strengthen

S1 Outline the stages by which the Hundred Flowers campaign developed.

S2 Give three reasons why Mao introduced the 'Anti-Rightist' purge.

S3 Describe two features of the 'Anti-Rightist' purge.

Challenge

C1 Explain two ways in which the 'Anti-Rightist' purge benefited Mao.

C2 Outline one way in which the 'Anti-Rightist' purge differed from the earlier 'antis' movements.

How confident do you feel about your answers to these questions? Form a small group and discuss any questions you are not sure about. Look for the answers in this section. Now rewrite your answers as a group.

Recap: Establishing communist rule, 1945–59

Recall quiz

1 What does PLA stand for?
2 In what year did conflict between the GMD and the CCP become a full civil war again?
3 What is the definition of 'proletariat'?
4 Which Soviet leader died in 1953?
5 How many landlords died in the rural terror?
6 Which campaign was the main turning point in the Civil War?
7 Give two economic problems that undermined faith in the GMD during the Civil War.
8 Which leader did Mao scapegoat at the end of the Hundred Flowers campaign?
9 At which university did student protests start during the Hundred Flowers campaign?
10 What is the definition of 'patronage'?

Activities ?

1 Copy and complete the following table about the key changes that took place in China in the years 1945–57.

In 1945	In 1959
The leader of China was …	The leader of China was …
The CCP controlled …	The CCP controlled …
The problems affecting people in urban areas included …	The problems affecting people in urban areas included …
The majority of farms were owned by …	The majority of farms were owned by …
The majority of factories were owned by …	The majority of factories were owned by …

2 Make a quiz about the Civil War. Set 10 questions on the key military campaigns, the reasons for CCP victory, and the role of the two leaders.
   a The first seven questions should test knowledge of names, dates, facts and figures.
   b Two questions should ask about causes, beginning with the word 'Why'.
   c The last question should address the whole of the Civil War and requires evaluation, beginning with the words 'How far'.
3 Swap quizzes with a classmate and answer the questions.
4 Mark each other's quizzes and give feedback to each other.

Activity ?

Write Mao's end of term report: how successful was Mao in the years 1945–57? Include comments on Mao's achievements in terms of:
a military success
b control of China's cities
c control of rural China.
Now, for each section, give Mao a score on the following scale:
1 = Complete failure: no aims met.
2 = Largely a failure: majority of aims not met.
3 = Largely a success: majority of aims met.
4 = Complete success: all aims met.

Exam-style question, Section B

How far do you agree with Interpretation 4 (on page 37) about Mao's reasons for launching the 'Anti-Rightist' purge? Explain your answer, using Interpretations 4 and 5 and your own knowledge of the historical context.   **16 marks**

Exam tip

You should focus on the main argument of the interpretations, rather than the specific details contained in the interpretations.

Writing historically: organising ideas

The most successful historical writing is clearly organised, guiding the reader through the writer's ideas.

Learning outcomes

By the end of this lesson, you will understand how to:

- organise your ideas into paragraphs
- link your paragraphs to guide the reader.

Definitions

Paragraph: a unit of text that focuses on a particular point or idea and information related to it.

How can I organise my ideas into paragraphs?

Look at the notes below written in response to this exam-style question:

Explain why Mao launched the 'Anti-Rightist' purge in 1957. **(12 marks)**

Hundred Flowers campaign gets out of control

Pressure from senior members of the CCP

Mao worried about the way students were criticising the CCP

Mao wanted to purge bureaucrats from the CCP

Students publishing their own magazines

Mao's plan to weed out enemies of the CCP

Now look at the response below.

Mao launched the 'Anti-Rightist' purge because he wanted to end widespread criticism of the CCP. During the Hundred Flowers campaign, Mao allowed people to criticise his government. This led economists to criticise the first Five-Year Plan, and scientists and experts to criticise the way the CCP ran factories. Students went further and criticised Mao's rule of China. Students demanded freedom and democracy, which Mao did not want to allow. Therefore, Mao introduced the 'Anti-Rightist' purge to humiliate and imprison dangerous critics of his government.

There is also evidence that Mao had planned to launch the 'Anti-Rightist' purge. From 1949, Mao was worried that bureaucrats were taking over the CCP, and that there were still enemies of communism who had not been weeded out. Therefore, he launched the 'Anti-Rightist' purge to get rid of bureaucrats and the enemies of the CCP who had criticised the government during the Hundred Flowers campaign.

1. **a.** What is the key focus of each of these paragraphs?

   b. Why do you think this response chose to focus on these two key areas?

   c. Why do you think this response chose to sequence these two paragraphs in this order?

   d. Which points in the notes have not been included in the final response? Why do you think the writer decided not to include them?

2. Look closely at the structure of the first paragraph. Which sentences:

   a. clearly indicate the central topic of the paragraph

   b. show knowledge and understanding of that topic

   c. explain its significance to the question?

02 | Economic policy, 1949–65

Mao believed that establishing communism was about political and economic reform. Indeed, most Marxists believe that oppression and exploitation are caused by economic issues. Mao was committed to reforming the economy in order to create a free and equal society. He was also committed to industrialising China because, like most Marxists, he believed that socialism and communism were only possible in advanced industrial societies.

Mao's early policies were very successful. Early land reform policies, and the first steps towards collectivisation, led to increased agricultural production. They were also popular as they redistributed land to the peasants. Equally, China's first Five-Year Plan led to phenomenal growth in industrial production, leading to an increase in the urban workforce and a rise in the standard of living for the population.

However, after a successful start, Mao changed from a pragmatic policy which led to steady growth to a utopian policy that caused chaos and disaster. The Great Leap Forward and the people's communes were greeted with genuine enthusiasm by the Chinese people. Yet, Mao's ambitious policies led to a great famine which resulted in the deaths of 30 million people.

The failure of Mao's policies also had political consequences. Mao retired from active government and Liu Shaoqi and Deng Xiaoping adopted less ambitious polices which helped restore economic growth.

Learning outcomes

In this chapter, you will find out about:

- Mao's key economic ideas
- how the CCP reformed agriculture and industry
- why Mao's economic policy became more radical in 1958
- what happened during the Great Leap Forward and the great famine.

2.1 Early changes in agriculture, 1949–57

Between 1949 and 1957, Mao and the CCP introduced a series of reforms in agriculture. Mao wanted:

- agriculture to become more efficient
- to retain the support of the peasants
- to produce more food in order to feed the growing urban workforce and to sell overseas to raise money to fund industrialisation.

Generally speaking, the CCP's policies achieved Mao's aims. Agriculture became more efficient, peasants accepted Mao's policies willingly and food production tended to increase.

Timeline

Agricultural policy, 1949–57

- **1950** Agrarian Reform Law
- **1950** Attacks on landlordism begin
- **1951–52** Mutual Aid Teams (MATs) introduced
- **1953–54** Agricultural Producers' Co-operatives (APCs) introduced
- **1955–56** Advanced Agricultural Producers' Co-operatives (Advanced APCs) introduced
- **1957** Record grain harvests

Activity **?**

Read Source A. Design a poster to promote the CCP's land reform campaign.

a The poster should have five panels, one for each of the five articles listed.

b Each panel should have a picture showing how the policy is supposed to work, and a simple summary of the article.

Land reform

Mao was committed to redistributing farmland from landlords to the peasants. Land reform was an important ideological aim, as it was designed to create equality in the countryside and end the power of the landlord class. By October 1949, in the north, the CCP's redistribution of land meant that around 85% to 90% of farmers were working their own land. In the south, where the CCP was still establishing control, only around 45% of peasants owned the land they worked; the rest paid rent to landlords.

Source A

From a government proclamation setting out the basic programme of land reform. The proclamation was issued throughout southern China during the years 1949–50.

Article 1: The agrarian system of ... exploitation is abolished. The agrarian system of 'land to the tillers' is to be realised.

Article 2: Landownership rights of all landlords are abolished.

Article 4: All debts incurred in the countryside prior to ... [land reform] are cancelled.

Article 5: The legal executive organs [organisations] for the reform of the agrarian system shall be the village peasants' meetings, and the committees elected by them ...

Article 6: ... all land of landlords in the villages, and all public land, shall be taken over by the village peasants' associations [committees] ...

Attacks on landlordism

The CCP took a series of steps in 1949–50 to end the power of landlordism*. They included:

- **The Agrarian Reform Law of 1950.** The law aimed to end the power of landlords and to increase agricultural production. The law gave the CCP the right to take land away from landowners and give it to 'the tillers' – the peasants who worked the land.
- **Struggle meetings.** Local land reform committees organised 'struggle meetings' at which landlords were forced to admit their crimes in front of the whole community. Struggle meetings ensured that former landlords were humiliated. On some occasions they led to the execution of landlords.
- **Terror.** Mao tried to encourage a policy of slow and peaceful land reform. However, CCP work parties were permitted to use force. In some areas, violence was intense; in others, land reform was largely peaceful. Overall, around 1 million landlords were killed between 1950 and 1952.

Land reform stripped landlords, most of whom had been supporters of the GMD, of their power.

Key term

Landlordism*

A system in which a small number of more wealthy individuals owned land and made money by renting this land to poor rural individuals, who were in the majority.

Source B

From a report made by the vice chairman of the North Jiangsu Land Reform Committee in late 1950. Jiangsu was one of the territories that the CCP conquered in 1949.

```
The government adopted urgent measures, gave
support to the peasants' righteous struggles,
set up People's Courts and brought lawless
landlords under control. The [land reform]
movement merged with the 'Resist-America,
Support-Korea' and counter-revolutionary
campaigns and the enthusiasm of the masses
reached unprecedented heights. Blazing like
a fire set to a dry tinder, the struggle
systematically unfolded to become the high-
tide of the anti-feudal [anti-landlord] mass
movement.
```

Exam-style question, Section A

Give two things you can infer from Source B about the peasants' reaction to land reform in China in 1950. **4 marks**

Exam tip

You infer something from a source by working out something the source does not actually tell you directly. Remember to make an inference about the enquiry in the exam question.

The redistribution of land

By the summer of 1952, the programme of land reform had been largely completed. Estimates suggest that, between 1950 and 1952:

- around 40% of land had been redistributed
- around 60% of peasants had benefited from the redistribution of land.

Inequality in the countryside

- Levels of inequality in the countryside were radically reduced, as shown in Figure 2.1.

1950

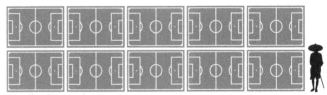

Poorest peasants = 0.4 hectares

Landlords = 8.0 hectares

1952

Poorest peasants = 0.8 hectares

Landlords = 1.5 hectares

Figure 2.1 The consequences of land reform, 1949–52.

Production

Redistribution of land was accompanied by the introduction of the Four Freedoms. These were the freedom to:

- buy, sell and rent land
- hire labour
- lend money
- trade.

The Four Freedoms helped lead to an increase in agricultural production because they allowed peasants to organise their own farms, and because trade gave peasants an incentive to work hard in order to make a profit. Therefore, between 1950 and 1952, agricultural production increased at 15% a year.

Problems in Chinese farming

Following land reform, there were still problems in farming:

- Land reform created small farms. However, large farms were more efficient, as resources could be shared.
- By 1953, China's total population, of around 582.6 million, had been increasing faster than food

Source C

A government poster created in 1951 by the CCP. The text says 'Another land reform benefit: a new ox on the farm'.

production. What is more, as China industrialised, the urban population grew. These urban areas needed more food.

These problems led Mao to introduce a new policy to make agriculture more efficient.

THINKING HISTORICALLY Cause and consequence (6a)

Seeing things differently

Different times and different places have different sets of ideas. Beliefs about how the world works, how human societies should be governed or the best way to achieve economic prosperity can all be radically different from our own. It is important for the historian to take into account these different attitudes when examining people's reactions and motivations in the past.

Land reform

During Mao's rule of China, land was redistributed from the rich to the poor. Mao was a socialist and he believed that working people should benefit most from the economy rather than those who simply owned property.

1   Imagine that the government in your country redistributed property to ensure everyone had a home.
   a   What would be the reaction of the media?
   b   What would be the reaction of the people who gained a home?
   c   What would be the reaction of those who lost some of their property?

2   Mao's attitudes to wealth and property were different to current attitudes in the UK.
   a   Write one sentence outlining Mao's government's beliefs about property. Write one sentence outlining the UK government's beliefs about property.
   b   Write one sentence outlining peasants' beliefs about property in Mao's China. Write one sentence outlining the beliefs about property of most ordinary people in the UK today.

3   Write a paragraph explaining how Mao's attitudes towards property contributed to land reform in the early 1950s. Remember to refer to the attitudes of the government and the peasants.

Moves towards agricultural co-operation

Mao's long-term vision for agriculture was to create efficient mechanised* collective farms*. Small private farms would be merged into larger farms and taken into government ownership, a process called collectivisation.

To retain the support of peasants, Mao acted carefully. Between December 1951 and 1957, he introduced a series of policies which encouraged peasants to co-operate while allowing them a large degree of economic freedom. Consequently, most peasants embraced the policies enthusiastically.

Key terms

Mechanised*

Something is mechanised when much of the work is done by machines rather than humans or animals.

Collective farms*

Large farms owned and run by the government.

Mutual Aid Teams

In 1951–52, the government began to encourage the establishment of Mutual Aid Teams (MATs). MATs were attractive to peasants for a number of reasons.

- Peasants continued to own the land that they worked.
- Peasants worked in teams of five to ten households, usually including their neighbours and extended families.
- Peasants shared tools and equipment, particularly at harvest time, making the farms more efficient.
- MATs were voluntary, so peasants could join or withdraw at any time.

By the end of 1952, around 40% of farmers had joined a MAT.

Agricultural Producers' Co-operatives

The second step towards collectivisation was the establishment of Agricultural Producers' Co-operatives (APCs) in 1953–54. They were voluntary, as Mao knew the peasants wanted to retain their independence.

Source D

A photograph taken by a CCP photographer in 1953 showing Mao meeting peasants, part of a MAT, during a visit to Nanjing in the south-east of China.

Farmers created APCs by pooling their land. Although farmers shared resources, they continued to own their land, animals and tools. Therefore, wealthy peasants were paid for sharing their resources with the rest of the APC. A peasant who withdrew from an APC could take their property with them. The creation of APCs made agriculture more efficient. It was also a step towards communism as it encouraged sharing.

APCs usually contained 20 to 30 households, which tended to be the whole of a village. Members of each APC were paid according to the work they did, which meant that there was an incentive to work hard.

Interpretation 1

From *Mao: A Very Short Introduction* by Delia Davin, published in 2013.

The pattern of initial moderation followed by radicalism seen in land reform also characterised the collectivisation of agriculture. … Agricultural collectivisation was supposed to start slowly relying on voluntarism. Peasants were to be encouraged to pool their efforts and resources through mutual aid teams which would then be a foundation for small-scale co-operatives. However, in 1955, difficulties in procuring enough grain to feed the rapidly growing urban population led the communist leadership to put heavy pressure on the peasants to enter co-operatives.

Activities ?

1 Read Interpretation 1. Use it to help draw a flow chart showing the stages through which collectivisation progressed from 1949 to 1955.

2 Design a poster urging peasants to join a co-operative.

3 List three ways in which the flow chart and poster do not tell the whole story of land reform up to 1955.

Source E

A photograph showing peasants working together to irrigate a field on an APC. The photograph was taken by a CCP photographer in November 1954 in Hunan province.

There was some resistance to the formation of APCs. In the first year, only 14% of peasants joined the APCs. This resistance, and widespread flooding in the spring of 1954, meant that there were grain shortages. In August 1955, the government was forced to introduce grain rationing. However, after a couple of years, the APCs proved to be more efficient than MATs. Consequently, farms produced a record harvest in 1956.

	Land reform	MATS	APCs	Advanced APCs
Size of farms (number of households)	1	5–10	20–30	150–200
Pooled property	None	Tools and animals, at harvest time	Land, tools and animals	Land, tools and animals

Figure 2.2 Agricultural policy, 1949–57.

Advanced APCs

The success of the APCs led the government to introduce Advanced APCs in 1955–56. Advanced APCs were larger than APCs, comprising between 150 and 200 households. They were also more socialist, and payments were no longer given on the land or resourced shared, merely on the amount of work done. Advanced APCs remained voluntary and farmers could take their property back.

The Advanced APCs led to a further growth in production. The Advanced APCs were popular: by early 1957, almost 90% of peasants had joined Advanced APCs.

Activities ?

1 Write the headline for an article on the benefits of co-operation for peasants.

2 Underneath your headline, list the main points you would want to make in the article.

3 Choose one point and write a short paragraph on it.

Success to 1957

Between 1949 and 1957, the CCP's land reform and then the moves towards agricultural co-operation led to a steady growth in production. Additionally, after the campaign against landlordism, resistance to government policy in the countryside had been limited. Land reform persuaded the vast majority of peasants that the government was on their side, and they recognised the benefits of working co-operatively.

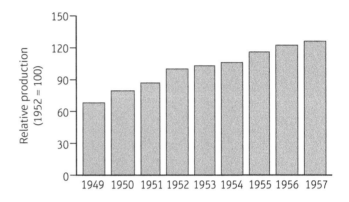

Figure 2.3 Agricultural production, 1949–57.

Summary

- The CCP's initial policy of land reform redistributed farmland to peasants.
- Between 1951 and 1957, the CCP introduced a series of reforms which encouraged farmers to share tools, land and labour.
- Farm production grew between 1949 and 1957.
- Steps towards collectivisation were largely peaceful in the early part of CCP rule.

Checkpoint

Strengthen

S1 Describe the differences between Chinese agriculture in 1949 and 1957.

S2 Define MATs, APCs and Advanced APCs.

S3 Explain the meaning of collectivisation.

Challenge

C1 Summarise the aims of CCP agricultural policy in the period 1949–57.

C2 Evaluate the extent to which CCP agricultural policy achieved its aims by 1957.

How confident do you feel about your answers to these questions? If you are not sure you answered them well, form a group with other students, discuss the answers and then record your conclusions. Your teacher can give you some hints.

2.2 The communes

In 1958, the CCP introduced people's communes, huge collective farms. These communes were part of the Great Leap Forward, a radical attempt to transform China.

Timeline

Agriculture in China, 1957–60

- **1957** Four Pests campaign
- **1958** Introduction of communes
- **1958** Lysenkoism introduced
- **1958** Beginning of great famine
- **1959–60** Droughts in Sichuan, Shandong and Henan provinces
- **1960** Rationing introduced
- **1960** Introduction of emergency policies and reform of communes

Radicalisation, 1958

The radicalisation of policy which occurred in 1958 came about because:

- The CCP wanted to increase agricultural production through an irrigation* programme. CCP leaders argued for the creation of larger farms which would have the resources to invest in irrigation.
- Mao was concerned that China's revolution risked losing momentum. He believed that the CCP had become increasingly bureaucratic* and had lost its revolutionary spirit.

Establishing the communes

Mao announced the new policy of communes in August 1958. Two new slogans explained Mao's ideas:

- **'Walking on two legs'.** The slogan meant that, in order to make progress, the economy needed to develop both agriculture and industry.
- **'Politics in charge'.** This slogan emphasised the importance of political will. Mao argued that previous policies had been too cautious because they had focused on what was possible in terms of economic theories. Mao argued that the CCP could achieve more by trusting the political will of the people.

The first people's commune, called the Sputnik Commune, was established in August 1958. Within four months, 26,000 communes had been established, covering 99% of China's farms.

Extend your knowledge

Sputnik

Sputnik was the world's first artificial satellite. It was launched by Soviet space scientists in 1957. Communist leaders argued that Sputnik showed that communism was more technically advanced than capitalism. China's first commune was named after Sputnik as a symbol that the communes, like the satellite, were more advanced than capitalist agriculture.

Key terms

Irrigation*

The process of creating artificial rivers and canals, on farmland, in order to improve water supply and to increase crop growth.

Bureaucratic*

Dominated by rules and government officials.

Source A

A photograph taken by a CCP photographer showing peasants working on a rice field in Guangdong province. The photograph was taken in September 1958 at one of the first communes, which was set up as a model for the rest of Chinese agriculture.

The organisation of the communes

The new communes were radically different from the co-operatives. First, they were much bigger, some containing as many as 5,000 households. Secondly, the communes were responsible for producing industrial goods as well as food. Finally, unlike the co-operatives, the communes were compulsory.

Source B

A government photograph showing peasants eating together in a communal canteen in 1958.

Exam-style question, Section A

Explain why the CCP introduced communes in 1958. You may use the following in your answer:

- agricultural production
- Mao's ideology.

You **must** also use information of your own. **12 marks**

Exam tip

Question 2 will always suggest two points that you could discuss in your answer. You may want to use one or both. Significantly, in order to get more than 8 marks, you must go beyond the two suggested points. Therefore, you should always include at least one point from your own knowledge.

Life in the communes

Life in the communes reflected communist principles. Peasants were required to give their animals, tools and land to the commune. Each commune had many common features.

- **Childcare was organised by the commune.** Therefore, most women were able to work.
- **Food was provided freely in communal canteens**. Peasants could eat as much as they liked, regardless of how hard they worked.
- **Commune workers were expected to work extremely long days.** The working day was usually 12 hours long, but at harvest time it increased to 18 hours.

- **Members of the commune were expected to be part of a militia.** All members between 15 and 50 years of age were required to undertake regular military training. Military discipline was supposed to be at the heart of the way people worked in the communes.
- **The militia units formed the police force in the communes.** They policed all aspects of commune life. For example, they punished people who did not work hard enough.
- **Peasants were encouraged to do non-agricultural work.** For example, male peasants were encouraged to take part in making steel in backyard furnaces, as well as creating irrigation systems.

Extend your knowledge

Militias in the communes
A militia is made up of working people, whereas a regular army is made up of professional soldiers. Karl Marx believed that, in a communist society, the army would be replaced by a militia of the people. This is one of the reasons why the CCP encouraged militias within the communes.

Source C

A government photograph showing peasants digging irrigation trenches on a commune during 1958.

Irrigation in 1957, 58 and 64			
	1957	**1958**	**1964**
Total area of new farmland irrigated (million hectares)	4,160	8,000	3,840

Extend your knowledge

Communes and communism
During 1958, Mao seems to have believed that the communes were the ideal form of human organisation. Mao argued that the communes had the potential to abolish money, gender inequality, exploitation and even government.

Problems with the communes

Initially, peasants were enthusiastic about the communes. They trusted that Mao's idea would lead them towards communism, a society in which they would all be wealthy and have plentiful leisure time. However, over time, problems emerged with the communes.

By the autumn of 1958, the problems were becoming obvious. Lower rates of production and poor administration meant that national food shortages started to become an issue.

Activities ?

1 Write down two main reasons why Mao was so keen to introduce communes.

2 Make a table with two columns. The first column, headed 'Improve life', should list how the introduction of the communes might improve life in China. The second column, headed 'Make life worse', should list how communes might make life worse.

3 Hold a class debate on the proposition 'The communes were bound to fail'. Afterwards, write down your own opinion about how likely the communes were to fail.

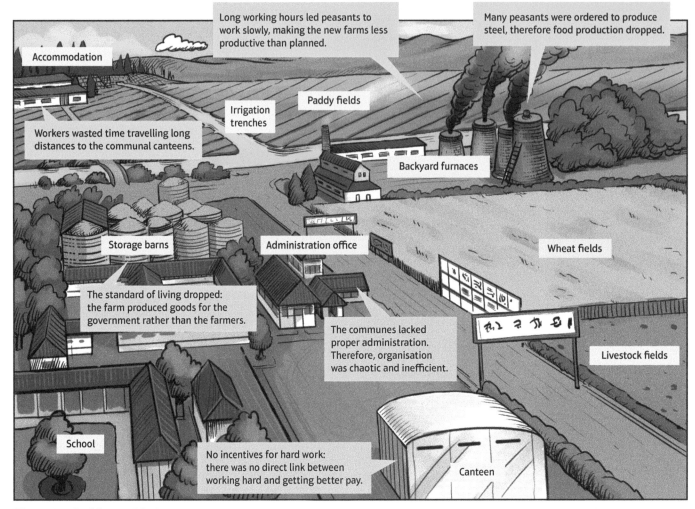

Figure 2.4 Problems with the communes.

Source D

An extract from the recollections of Qui Wenhua, recorded in 2013 in an oral history of the great famine that affected China. Qui was nine years old at the time he joined the commune. He lived in Henan province, which was primarily rural.

In 1959 I was still at school. Every day we had to listen to things like mass production of iron and steel. I had no idea what they meant. Men and women, all ... labourers, were told to go into the river to dig sand because someone said the sand ... had a high iron content. ... There was no one at home to harvest the crops ... They were left to rot in the field ...

At the time we were told that we had entered into Communism, and there would be no more private housing. ... our house was turned into a granary ...

Source E

From an official report from the Red Flag People's Commune, located in the Qinghai province of central China. The report describes the period in which the Advanced APCs were merged to create the commune, and was written in late 1958.

One day when small brigade No. 12 ... held a meeting ... the commune members registered their orchards, houses, sheep, household chairs, tables, boards, benches, pots and stoves, together with their production material ... and wholeheartedly handed them over to the commune. We asked some commune members: how shall you later buy radios and watches ...? If you can, will they be considered the commune's? They didn't hesitate to answer ... whatever belongs to private individuals must be ... useful to the development of production.

Declining production

CCP leaders had hoped that the communes would lead to greater efficiency and therefore greater production. However, agricultural production declined. Wheat and rice production fell every year from 1957 to 1961, and grain production rose only slightly in 1958 before falling away. Inefficiencies in the communes and the lack of incentives for hard work played a role in this fall. However, there were other forces at work, including Lysenkoism and the Four Pests Campaign.

Grain production 1957–61					
Year	1957	1958	1959	1960	1961
Grain production (million metric tons)	195.0	200.0	170.0	143.5	147.5

The significance of Lysenkoism

Lysenkoism was a pseudoscientific* movement which was extremely influential in the USSR and China in the late 1950s. The movement was based on the ideas of Trofim Lysenko, the director of the Soviet Academy of Agricultural Sciences.

Key term

Pseudoscientific*

Theories which are presented as though they are scientific, even though they are not confirmed by scientific research.

Lysenko developed a series of theories about crop growth. He claimed that farmers could create 'super crops' which were 16 times as productive as regular crops. His method was to:

- expose seeds to cold and damp conditions
- plant seeds deep underground
- plant seeds close together.

These techniques created very harsh conditions which, Lysenko argued, would force plants to become stronger and therefore produce more food. The CCP introduced Lysenkoism in late 1958 in order to boost production.

The failure of Lysenkoism

Lysenkoism was based on incorrect ideas and the methods failed. The methods wasted vast amounts of resources and huge amounts of labour.

- **The failure of close planting.** Usually, Chinese peasants planted around 1.5 million seeds per acre. However, close planting meant they planted up to 15 million per acre. The result was massive crop failure. Over 90% of the seeds were wasted.
- **The failure of deep planting.** Wheat seeds are usually planted a couple of centimetres below the surface of the soil. However, influenced by Lysenko, the CCP ordered that wheat should be planted 1.5 metres into the soil. This wasted huge amounts of labour as tens of millions of peasants spent months digging. Deep planting failed, as the crops did not grow.

Extend your knowledge

Deep ploughing led to soil erosion. This continued to have an impact on farming long after Lysenkoism was dropped. This is one of the reasons why agricultural production took a long time to recover.

The Four Pests Campaign

The Four Pests Campaign, launched in 1957, also led to a decline in crop production. It targeted four pests that the CCP believed were eating grain and spoiling food. Peasants were instructed to eradicate:

- flies
- rats
- mosquitoes
- sparrows.

The campaign had little impact on flies, rats or mosquitoes, but it did lead to sparrowcide: the mass killing of sparrows. Villages competed to kill sparrows. People chased sparrows and made loud noises, which kept the birds flying. Eventually the birds dropped dead from exhaustion.

Sparrowcide in 1957 led to a plague of caterpillars and locusts in 1958, pests that sparrows would ordinarily eat. As sparrows died, caterpillars and insects flourished and ate the crops.

Source F

From Peng Dehuai's 'Letter of opinion'. Peng sent the letter to Mao privately during the Lushan Conference, a meeting of senior CCP officials. The meeting took place in July 1959 in order to discuss the progress of the communes and the Great Leap Forward. After Mao read the letter, he humiliated and sacked Peng.

First, the habit to exaggerate spread rather universally. Last year ... a higher estimate of grain production was made than was warranted. This created a false impression: everybody felt that the problem of food had been solved, and that our hands were free to engage in industry. ... At the time, from reports sent in from all directions, it would seem that communism was just around the corner. This caused not a few comrades to become hot in their brain. In the wave of high grain and cotton production and the doubling of iron and steel production, extravagance and waste developed.

Source G

From the *Peking Review*, 5 January 1962. The *Peking Review* was the weekly magazine of Chinese news published by the CCP.

Thanks to the organisation of the people's communes and their hard work the damage from the natural calamities was reduced to a minimum ... The Hsinkang People's Commune in Changsha, Hunan Province, was struck by both flood and drought last year. By extending its rice acreage, the commune was able to reap a bigger rice crop than in a normal year ...

The nation rejoiced at these achievements. They were won only after surmounting the difficulties brought about by three years of serious natural calamities.

The causes of the great famine, 1958–62

The fall in agricultural production continued into 1959, soon becoming one of the worst famines of the 20th century. The great famine of 1958–62 affected the whole country, leading to as many as 30 million deaths. Agricultural production did not recover fully from the crisis until 1984. The CCP attempted to cover up the disaster, and there was no appeal for international help. Indeed, the government continued exporting grain during the crisis and refused to acknowledge the crisis publicly until 1980.

The causes of the famine have been a subject of intense historical debate. There are a number of theories regarding the possible causes of the famine, all of which have problems.

Theory 1: Bad weather

The government refused to admit that there was famine. However, it did admit there were problems and blamed them on bad weather in 1959–61.

There was some bad weather during the great famine:

- In Sichuan, Shandong and Henan provinces, there were droughts in 1959 and 1960.
- There was heavy rain in Guangxi in 1959.

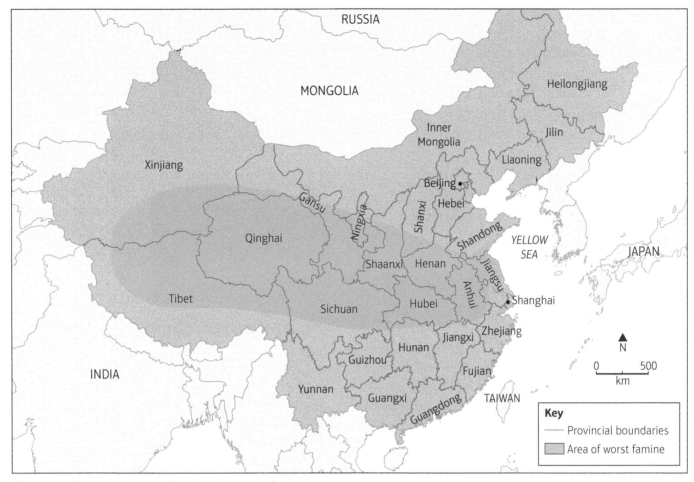

Figure 2.5 The areas worst affected by the great famine.

However, there are problems with this explanation.

- There were famine-affected areas where the weather was good or where bad weather was short-lived.
- Estimates suggest that the dry season in Sichuan was only responsible for around 12% of the drop in agricultural production in 1959.

Theory 2: Bad policies

A second theory is that government policies caused the famine. For example, some historians argue that Lysenkoism and the Four Pests Campaign were responsible.

Again, there are problems with this explanation. The CCP spotted problems with both of these policies and therefore both were stopped in 1959. The famine, however, continued until 1962.

Theory 3: The communes

Another theory is that the way communes were organised led to falling production which, in turn, led to famine.

However, reforms in 1959 and 1960 addressed many of these problems and yet the famine continued until 1962.

Theory 4: Central government

Other historians blame central government for the famine.

- By 1958, Mao was so feared that no one dared to criticise his policies. Rather, government officials hid evidence of economic problems to avoid being punished.
- The 'Anti-Rightist' purge (see page 36) had led to many experts, such as economists and statisticians, being expelled from the government. As a result, the government did not have the expertise to administer the new communes or to understand the impact of its policies.

- The radicalisation of Mao's ideology in 1958 meant that the CCP introduced utopian policies which were essentially unworkable.
- Mao refused to accept offers of help from other countries because he did not want to admit his policies had failed.
- The CCP exported almost 7 million tons of grain in 1959 in order to buy machinery to invest in industrial development.

There are problems with this interpretation, as central government introduced rationing in 1960 to try and address the food shortages.

Interpretation 1

From *Food Security and Farm Land Protection in China* by Yushi Mao, published in 2012.

Severe natural disasters with 'an unprecedented disaster area in the 1950s' occurred throughout the country in 1959. … The drought area of Henan, Shandong, Sichuan, Anhui, Hubei, Hunan and Heilongjiang accounted for 82.9% of the total damaged area throughout the country.

After the disasters in 1959, extraordinarily serious natural disasters which were rarely seen in the last century occurred in most regions …

The natural disasters in 1960 not only affected a larger area than before but also happened continuously on the basis of disasters in 1959. Therefore, fatal damages were caused.

Interpretation 2

From *The People's Republic of China 1949–76* by Michael Lynch, published in 2010.

But poor weather does not explain the famine. It is true that 1958 was a bad year, although not particularly exceptional by Chinese standards. However, the weather in the following 3 years was notably mild. Whatever Mao might claim, the famine was not a misfortune of nature; it was a direct and fatal consequence of the decisions he took.

Exam-style question, Section B

Suggest **one** reason why Interpretations 1 and 2 give different views about the causes of the great famine of 1959–61.

You may use Sources F and G to help explain your answer. **4 marks**

Exam tip

In order to do well in this question, you must give a reason why the interpretations disagree and support that reason. Simply stating a reason will not get you the highest marks.

The impact of the great famine

The great famine had huge social consequences, including causing an enormous loss of life. In Sichuan province, for example, approximately 9 million people out of 62 million died, and in Henan 7.8 million of the 44.4 million inhabitants died.

Starvation

Starvation was worse in rural areas. The government seized grain in the countryside in order to feed the urban population. Food consumption dropped by 25% in the countryside, whereas it dropped by around 8% in cities. As a result, death rates in rural areas were higher than death rates in cities.

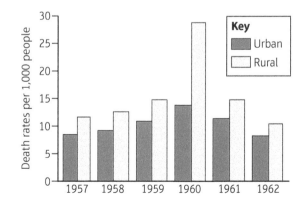

Figure 2.6 Death rates per 1,000 people, 1957–62.

THINKING HISTORICALLY ▶ Interpretations (4b)

Method is everything

A spectrum of historical methodology

Bad history
- Based on gut feeling
- Argument does not progress logically
- No supporting evidence

Good history
- Based on an interpretation of evidence
- Argument progresses logically
- Evidence used to support argument

Student conclusion 1

Overall, I feel that the communes were to blame for the terrible famine. People should not be forced to give up their property and live together. Governments should not introduce utopian policies like the communes. Governments have a duty to make sure that everyone has enough to eat; they have no right to force people to transition to socialism.

Student conclusion 2

Therefore, communes were introduced in 1958 as part of a major policy change by Mao. The communes were more radical than the Advanced APCs and introduced communal eating and childcare, as well as backyard furnaces. The famine began soon afterwards, and 30 million people died.

Student conclusion 3

In conclusion, government policies were largely responsible for the famine. Bad polices such as Lysenkoism wasted a large amount of resources, including labour. The Four Pests Campaign also led to an increase in crop-eating insects due to sparrowcide, which killed their predators. Therefore, government policies caused the famine as they were wasteful and led to the destruction of crops.

Work in pairs. Read the above conclusions to the question 'How far were government policies responsible for the great famine?' and answer the questions.

1   Look at all the conclusions. In what ways do they differ from one another?

2   Look carefully at the spectrum of historical methodology.

   a   Where would you place each student's conclusion on the spectrum?

   b   What evidence would you use to support your choice?

   c   Suggest one improvement to each conclusion that would move it towards 'good' historical writing.

3   How important is it that we know what to look for when we are reading and evaluating historical writing?

Attempts at survival

In rural areas, peasants tried various methods to survive, including attacking grain stores. The authorities responded with brutal punishments, and 12.5% of the population were punished for food crimes. Without trial, peasants were executed or had their fingers or hands cut off. Children caught stealing food were suspended from fences by wires that were forced through their ears.

Peasants used a variety of methods to survive. These included:

- eating rats or worms
- making porridge from tree bark and leaves
- cannibalism: some people ate dead bodies; children were kidnapped, killed and eaten
- some women resorted to prostitution in order to survive
- the practice of parents selling their daughters also re-emerged, in order to raise money
- children also left school in order to forage for food or work on farms.

Survival strategies undermined CCP objectives, including education and the advancement of women's rights. The authorities punished instances of cannibalism severely.

Source H

A photograph by a foreign journalist showing starving peasants arriving in a city in search of food. The photograph was taken during the great famine.

Decollectivisation

Communes began to disintegrate due to the famine. Decollectivisation happened most quickly and thoroughly in areas which had been worst affected by the famine, such as Sichuan and Anhui.

Activity ?

Imagine you are an adviser to the Chinese government. Draw a table with two columns.

a In the first column, list the problems facing China in 1960. Make sure you list at least three key problems.

b In the second column, suggest a series of solutions, at least one for every problem. You should explain how your ideas will solve each problem.

Social impact

- Huge loss of life – 30 million deaths.
- Widespread starvation.
- Increase in crime and breakdown of order.
- Survival strategies, such as children leaving school to find food or work, undermine education and women's rights.

Economic impact

- Disruption of the economy.
- Decollectivisation of farms and restoration of private farming.
- Peasants allowed to trade food.
- Reform of communes.
- Need to import wheat.

Great famine

Political impact

- Mao loses authority.
- Liu Shaoqi and Deng Xiaoping take over economic policy.
- Abandonment of Mao's policies and adoption of pragmatic policies.

Figure 2.7 Social, economic and political impact of the great famine.

Reasons for the restoration of private farming

The great famine also had political and economic consequences. Liu Shaoqi and Deng Xiaoping (who had briefly been minister of finance in 1953–54) took over Party economic policy. Liu and Deng abandoned Mao's ideological policies and introduced pragmatic policies designed to end the famine. The restoration of private farming was an essential part of their programme.

Emergency reforms

Between July and November 1960, Liu and Deng introduced a series of temporary emergency policies to deal with the famine.

- Soldiers, students and unemployed people were sent to villages to work on farms.
- Peasants were allowed to own small private farms in order to grow food. Around 18% of China's farmland was decollectivised.
- Peasants were allowed to trade any spare food.
- Prisoners in labour camps had to make farm tools.
- New fertilisers and tools were sent to the countryside to help encourage efficient farming.

Liu and Deng hoped that the reintroduction of private farming would give farmers an incentive to grow more in order to ensure they made a profit.

Reform of the communes

During the famine, communes had begun to break down. Liu and Deng introduced new reform policies.

- Communes were no longer required to make industrial goods: their priority was to produce food.
- Communes were reduced to 1,600 households.
- Production within each commune was organised in teams of about 20–30 households.
- Pay and other benefits were linked clearly to work, so that hard work was rewarded.
- Communal canteens were finally phased out.

Agricultural recovery

Liu and Deng's policies led to the recovery of agriculture. Grain production grew from 147.5 million tons in 1961 to 214.0 million tons in 1966. In the short term, the recovery was slow, and therefore Liu and Deng authorised large imports of wheat from abroad.

Activities ?
1 Make a timeline of Chinese farming covering the period 1949–65.
2 Draw a line on the timeline to represent the rise and fall of production.
3 Annotate the timeline, explaining why the rises and falls occurred.

Summary

- The introduction of communes was a bold policy designed to speed up China's transition to communism.
- Life in the communes reflected the communist principle of sharing property and wealth.
- The communes and other policies, such as Lysenkoism, led to reduced production and waste of resources.
- Historians disagree over the prime cause of the 1958–62 great famine, that led to up to 30 million deaths.

Checkpoint

Strengthen

S1 Describe the key features of the communes.

S2 List three problems caused by the creation of the communes.

S3 List the four main theories that explain the causes of the great famine.

Challenge

C1 Summarise two of Mao's main reasons for introducing the communes.

C2 Summarise the reasons for the failure of Lysenkoism.

If you are not sure about your answers, go back to the text in this section to find the details you need.

2.3 Industry and the Five-Year Plan, 1953–57

Learning outcomes

- Understand Mao's reasons for launching the first Five-Year Plan.
- Learn about the way the Plan worked.
- Find out about the impact of the first Five-Year Plan on China's economy.

Mao wanted to build a strong industrial nation. He believed this was essential to military strength, which would ensure that China was never again humiliated by a foreign power. Additionally, Mao believed, like most Marxists, that socialism could only be achieved through industrialisation.

The CCP's goal of industrialisation was clear. However, in 1949, there was no agreement on how to industrialise.

- Some communists argued that there should be a period of managed capitalism*, in which the national bourgeoisies were free to own factories and trade in order to push forward China's economic development.
- Other communists argued that China should take control of industrialisation by controlling factories and planning production.

Key term

Managed capitalism*

An economic system in which a capitalist market is allowed to operate. However, aspects of the market are controlled in order to achieve goals set by the government.

Timeline
Industry, 1950–57

February 1950 Mao and Stalin agree the Treaty of Friendship, Alliance and Mutual Assistance

November 1952 CCP establishes the State Planning Commission to develop first Five-Year Plan

October 1950 China's involvement in the Korean War leads to an international trade embargo

1953 Launch of first Five-Year Plan

1957 Mao's authority strengthened by perceived success of first Five-Year Plan

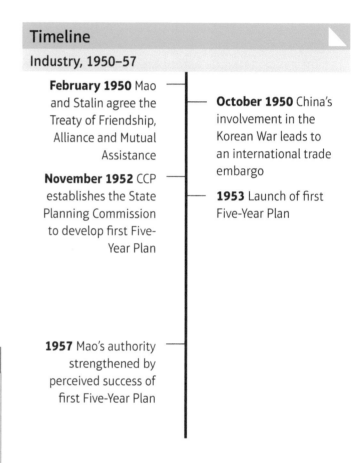

Reasons for the first Five-Year Plan

The CCP introduced the first Five-Year Plan for a number of reasons.

The success of the Soviet economy

Mao was impressed by the apparent success of the Soviet economy. In 1928, when Stalin had introduced the USSR's first Five-Year Plan, the Soviet economy had been largely rural, with a very small industrial sector. However, by 1941, Stalin's Five-Year Plans had transformed the USSR into an industrial power.

Capitalist economies, by comparison, had been less impressive. The USA, France, Britain, Germany and other major capitalist economies had all been hit hard by the Great Depression in 1929. For Mao, history indicated the superiority of Soviet-style planning over Western capitalism.

The Korean War and international embargo

Initially, the CCP was prepared to work with the national bourgeoisies (see page 30). Indeed, in 1949, Mao had promised China's capitalists at least 50 years of freedom to trade and do business.

However, the Korean War had demonstrated the vulnerability of Mao's new communist regime.

- During the war, US forces had come close to the Chinese border, and Mao had feared that the USA was planning to invade and overthrow the government.
- Fourteen western nations introduced a trade embargo* on China. Therefore, there was little hope of developing China's economy through trade. Consequently, a Soviet-style planned economy seemed the only option for China's leaders.

Therefore, Mao rethought his economic policy, and in 1953 he introduced China's first Five-Year Plan.

Key term

Embargo*

A ban on trade with another country. Embargos are usually introduced for political reasons. Trade restrictions can be total – a ban on all goods – or partial – a ban on some goods.

Efficiency

Mao also believed that economic planning was highly efficient. He knew that China had very limited resources and therefore wanted to use them as efficiently as possible.

Women's labour

The government believed that women had a key role to play in modernising the economy. Government campaigns encouraged women to work in factories, emphasising their equality with men. Broadly, government policy led to equal pay for men and women who did the same work. In that sense the policy was a success, as it achieved Mao's aim of gender equality. Nonetheless, men tended to be promoted into management jobs to a greater extent than women. Therefore, true gender equality in the workplace was not achieved.

Soviet aid

Soviet economic aid also helped the CCP initiate the policy of state planning. In February 1950, Mao and Stalin had agreed the Treaty of Friendship, Alliance and Mutual Assistance. The Treaty committed the USSR to provide loans to China and to provide resources and expertise in economic development. Mao believed that, with Soviet help, the CCP could create a planned economy similar to that of the USSR.

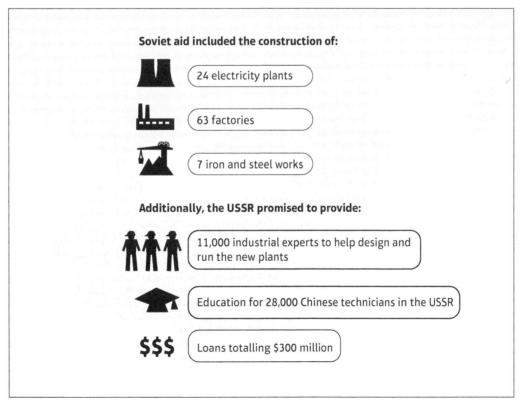

Figure 2.8 Soviet economic aid during the first Five-Year Plan.

Source A

From a March 1953 edition of *People's China*, a biweekly magazine printed in English and published by the CCP. The magazine was designed to spread news of Chinese achievements to Western nations.

'... the 1953 budget shows that our country has entered a new stage of large-scale and planned economic construction which is centred round the development of industry, first and foremost, heavy industry.'

The new stage of economic construction which began this year has become possible because of the impressive achievements in rehabilitation [economic reconstruction] since the founding of the Chinese People's Republic in 1949. ...

The great achievements of the Chinese people ... once again prove the superiority of the state and economic system of the People's Democracy [PRC] over that of capitalism.

Activities ?

1   In groups, discuss the factors leading to the launch of the first Five-Year Plan.

2   What reasons does Source A give for the introduction of the first Five-Year Plan?

3   Choose the reason that you think is the most significant and write a sentence explaining your choice.

The targets of the first Five-Year Plan

The overall goal of the first Five-Year Plan was to lay the foundation for a fully modern industrial economy. In practice, this meant focusing on heavy industry*. In this way, China's first Five-Year Plan was similar to the Soviet plans, which had emphasised the production of raw materials* such as:

- iron
- steel
- coal
- oil.

Indeed, almost 90% of Chinese government investment was directed at heavy industry. Light industry* received just over 10% of investment, reflecting the low priority of producing consumer goods. The Plan also aimed to **improve China's transport infrastructure** by building new roads, railways, bridges and canals – partly so the CCP could get PLA soldiers, government officials and Party officials across the whole of China – and to **increase the production of electricity**. The targets of the first Five-Year Plan were determined by a State Planning Commission, set up in 1952.

The Plan also aimed to **develop the economy in a comprehensive way**. Traditionally, Chinese industry had developed in coastal towns, because foreign countries had chosen to invest in trading ports. Mao and the CCP wanted the industrial economy to develop across the whole of China. Therefore, economic planners decided to establish almost 500 factories in China's interior, where there had been very little industrial development.

New ministries to control the production of coal, oil and steel were created. The Plan organised the production of 729 products including raw materials, essential items of clothing, bicycles and wristwatches.

Key terms

Heavy industry*

Economic production that requires large factories and large-scale industrial machinery. Heavy industry produces raw materials, such as iron and steel, and energy sources, such as coal and oil.

Raw materials*

Basic materials, such as metals, rubber and wood, which are used to produce more sophisticated goods.

Light industry*

Economic production that is based in relatively small workshops or factories. Rather than producing raw materials, light industry produces consumer goods, such as furniture, pots and pans and clothing.

The significance of the USSR's support

Aid from the USSR certainly helped the development of the first Five-Year Plan. However, Soviet expertise was much more important than Soviet money.

Soviet financial aid

Only 3% of the money invested during the first Five-Year Plan came from the USSR. The remaining 97% of the funds to develop Chinese industry came from China itself.

Soviet aid was also less helpful than anticipated. By the end of the Plan it was clear that the USSR had only completed around 45% of the 156 industrial enterprises that it had promised to build. What is more, Soviet loans were relatively expensive in terms of the interest* that China had to pay.

Soviet technical support

The USSR's technical support was more helpful. Soviet technicians had genuine industrial expertise, which helped Chinese planners to use resources effectively. Additionally, the USSR provided detailed plans for factories and machinery, which Chinese authorities were able to use as a basis for their own construction programme.

Key term
Interest*
The money paid to a lender for receiving a loan.

Source B

A Chinese government poster published in 1953. The text says 'Study the Soviet Union's advanced economy to build up our nation.'

Achievements of the first Five-Year Plan

In general terms, the first Five-Year Plan was extremely successful. However, the Plan did not meet all of its targets, nor did it develop the economy in a rounded way.

Successes of the first Five-Year Plan

Industry grew at around 16% a year. This exceeded the 14.7% target set by the State Planning Commission. Total industrial production doubled, and heavy industrial production almost tripled.

The first Five-Year Plan, 1953–57				
Industry	1952 production	Planned target	1957 production	Percentage of target achieved
Coal (million metric tons, mmt)	68.50	113.00	130.00	115
Oil (mmt)	436.00	2,012.00	1,458.00	73
Steel (mmt)	1.35	4.12	5.35	130
Electricity (billion kWh)	7.26	15.90	19.34	122

Key terms

Transition to socialism*

The process of modernising the economy and transforming society to create socialism.

Nationalise*

To transfer property from private ownership to state or national ownership.

Source C

A photograph taken by French photographer Marc Riboud, showing the construction of the Wuhan Yangtze River Bridge with Soviet technical assistance. The photograph was taken in March 1957.

Additionally, the urban population increased by 4 million. This was a success, as the CCP wanted to encourage the growth of the urban proletariat, as part of the transition to socialism*. Towns and cities expanded, and many workers benefited from better housing.

Other infrastructure was also improved. For example, the huge Wuhan Yangtze River Bridge (across the Yangtze River) and the Erling irrigation canals were constructed as a result of the Plan. Around 6,000 kilometres of railway line was built, connecting cities on the coast to cities far inland, in the northwest and southwest. Another transport achievement was the manufacture of over 1 million bicycles.

A further success was the abolition of private industry. The CCP wanted to nationalise* industry as part of the transition to socialism. This was achieved by 1956, when the last privately owned factories were nationalised.

There were also improvements in the standard of living of urban workers during the Plan. The government was able to invest in health and education.

Source D

From Zhou Enlai's report to the National People's Congress in June 1957.

In our First Five-Year Plan for Development of National Economy, we correctly worked out programmes to co-ordinate socialist construction and transformation, and in 1956, along with the upsurge in socialist transformation, socialist construction advanced with giant strides. ...

As a result of increased production there has been an improvement in the people's living conditions in the course of our large-scale construction work. ...

In 1952 the average wage for all workers and employees was 446 yuan [the Chinese currency] a year, but in 1956 this had risen to 610 yuan, an increase of nearly 37 per cent in four years.

Source E

From the *Times* newspaper, published in June 1957.

Peking [Beijing] may still put on an air of confidence and unruffled expansion to the outside world, but within China a mood of caution and scarcely concealed misgiving is apparent in this last year of the first Five-year Plan. The thousands who come from all over the country to conferences in Peking are being told of slower industrialisation, humbler objectives and renewed austerity. ...

... A long-delayed and inevitable wage increase for the industrial worker meant a suddenly increased demand for food and clothing which could not be fully met.

Failures of the Plan

The first Five-Year Plan was not wholly successful.

- **It failed to meet the target for oil production.** As a result, China still had to import huge amounts of oil.

- **It failed to meet targets for more complicated goods.** For example, industry made only 30% of the shipping and about 80% of the railway locomotives that had been planned.

- **Heavy industry grew dramatically, but light industry grew much more slowly.** While this was not regarded as a failure by planners, who had always intended to prioritise heavy industry, Mao began to emphasise the need for light industry in the run-up to a second Five-Year Plan.

- **Living standards in rural areas did not improve.** China paid for Soviet aid with grain, which meant the government needed large amounts of cheap grain. Therefore, the government imposed higher taxes on peasants and kept the price it paid for grain low. As a result, although the economy grew, China's peasants did not benefit.

- **Living standards for Chinese workers rose slowly.** In order to maximise investment in industry, the government put off a pay rise for urban workers until 1956. This led to strikes in China's cities in 1956.

- **There were inefficiencies in light industry.** The Plan was inefficient because it specified what kind of raw material each factory should receive but, crucially, it did not specify the quality. For example, light industrial plants often received steel in the wrong thickness or the wrong strength. This hampered the production of consumer goods, which remained scarce.

- **Mao was concerned that the Soviet style of planning was very centralised and inflexible.** He thought it created a new group of industrial experts who were becoming wealthier than ordinary workers.

Activity ?

1 Form two teams and play 'history tennis':

a Team 1 'serves' a success of the first Five-Year Plan at Team 2.

b Team 2 has to respond by 'returning serve' with a failure of the Plan.

c Continue playing for as long as you can.

d The team which is unable to come up with a success or failure loses the match.

Source F

A government photograph showing female workers in a tool plant. The photograph was taken as part of a campaign to encourage workers to beat the targets that they had been set.

Interpretation 1

From *China 1900–76* by Geoff Stewart, published in 2006.

The plan ran from 1953 to 1957 and seems to have been an extraordinary success. ... Coal production virtually doubled and electric power nearly tripled. Steel production quadrupled. There were more ships and locomotives and a staggering increase in the number of bicycles manufactured. Here were the first steps on the road to industrial transformation.

Mao's authority

The success of the Plan consolidated Mao's authority within the government. By 1957, Mao was credited as the leader who had beaten the GMD in the Civil War, who had inflicted defeats on the USA in the Korean War, and who had begun the industrialisation of China.

Mao's growing prestige had important political consequences. First, Mao felt secure enough to initiate the Hundred Flowers campaign (see page 32), and allow brief liberalisation. Secondly, Mao was emboldened to advocate a much more radical programme of reform called the Great Leap Forward (the second Five-Year Plan).

Interpretation 2

From *Demystifying the Chinese Economy* by Justin Yifu Lin, published in 2012.

The equipment industry in northeast China was supposed to get steel from An Steel, and Wuhan city was supposed to be supplied by Wu Steel. But a mismatch frequently took place. Why? Because only a couple of officials in the former State Planning Commission were designated to be in charge of steel, and they were overwhelmed by the large number of enterprises and their varied and complicated demands.

Activities

Read Interpretations 1 and 2.

1 Summarise the view of Interpretation 1.
2 Make a bullet point list of the facts it uses to support its view.
3 Make a bullet point list of facts that challenge the view of Interpretation 1. Include at least three facts in the list.

Exam-style question, Section B

Study Interpretations 1 and 2. They give different views about the success of China's first Five-Year Plan, 1953–57.

What is the main difference between the views?

Explain your answer, using details from both interpretations. **4 marks**

Exam tip

When answering a question about how interpretations differ, be sure to quote details from both of them to support what you say, or you will lose marks.

Summary

- CCP leaders believed that economic planning was the key to developing industry.
- The first Five-Year Plan focused on developing heavy industry.
- The first Five-Year Plan was broadly successful, as it led to the growth of industry and industrial production.
- Some targets were missed and living standards in the countryside failed to improve.
- The successes of the Plan boosted Mao's authority.

Checkpoint

Strengthen

S1 Describe the aims of the first Five-Year Plan.

S2 Give three reasons for the CCP's decision to launch the first Five-Year Plan.

S3 Summarise Mao's vision for Chinese industry.

Challenge

C1 Write a paragraph evaluating the success of the first Five-Year Plan.

C2 Explain how the successes of the first Five-Year Plan affected Mao's authority within the CCP.

If you are not sure about your answers, work with a friend. Swap work and see if you can think of ways of improving what you have each done.

2.4 Economic reform and the Great Leap Forward

Learning outcomes

- Understand Mao's reasons for the Great Leap Forward.
- Understand how the Great Leap Forward worked.
- Understand why the Great Leap Forward failed.
- Understand the extent and consequences of the failure of the Great Leap Forward.

The Great Leap Forward was a radical change from the first Five-Year Plan. Its goals were far more ambitious and its methods much more radical. Mao used the term 'leap' to indicate that China's aim was to overtake the British economy in terms of steel production within 15 years.

Mao's reasons for the second Five-Year Plan, 1958–62

Mao launched the second Five-Year Plan – the Great Leap Forward – because of problems with the first Five-Year Plan, China's relationship with the USSR, Mao's own ideology and China's resources.

Economic problems

The first Five-Year Plan had led to uneven economic growth. Heavy industry had grown massively, whereas agriculture and light industry had grown slowly. Therefore, Mao wanted a policy that would lead to balanced growth.

Unemployment had also become a problem. Mao wanted to solve the problem using China's greatest resource, its people, to achieve economic modernisation.

China and the USSR

Mao was also motivated by his increasingly tense relationship with the USSR. Following the death of Stalin in 1953, Mao became highly critical of the USSR. He believed that Khrushchev and the new Soviet leadership were bureaucrats who had lost their revolutionary spirit. Mao believed that the Five-Year Plans reflected this, as they relied on experts and bureaucrats rather than on the revolutionary energy of the people.

Additionally, the first Five-Year Plan had relied on the expertise of Soviet technicians and planners. Mao wanted a new policy which ended China's dependence on the USSR.

Mao's ideology

Mao was suspicious of experts, but had great faith in the peasants. Therefore, the Great Leap Forward emphasised the revolutionary energy of the Chinese people, rather than the plans of experts.

China's prestige

Mao was also concerned about China's international prestige. He wanted China to be a global power. Mao wanted a policy that would allow China to overtake Britain and show that China, rather than the USSR, was the leader of the communist world.

Source A

A photograph by a Western journalist showing backyard furnaces producing steel during 1958, the first year of the Great Leap Forward.

China's resources

Finally, Mao changed economic policy because Khrushchev cut Soviet aid. This forced Mao to devise a policy based on China's own resources and methods. China had a history of small-scale rural industry, in which peasants made steel in backyard furnaces. These were cheap and easy to build. Therefore, they did not require Soviet experts or aid. However, backyard furnaces required a great deal of labour. Mao hoped that mass mobilisation* of peasant labour, a key Chinese resource, would transform the economy.

Key term

Mass mobilisation*

A process of engaging large numbers of people in a single task.

Extend your knowledge

China, Britain and the USSR

Mao's goal of overtaking Britain was part of his goal that communism should overtake capitalism. In the late 1950s, Soviet leader Khrushchev set the goal that the Soviet economy would overtake the US economy. Mao believed that China should try and achieve a similar success by aiming to overtake Britain. In spite of Mao's utopianism, he realised that China would not overtake the USA for many decades.

Source B

A government poster produced in 1958. The text reads 'May the People's Communes Last for Ten Thousand Years!'

The Great Leap Forward

The Great Leap Forward was launched in mid-1958. Mao's aim was to achieve 'more, faster, better and more economical results'. It was radically different from the first Five-Year Plan. Rather than developing large-scale factories, based on the advice of Soviet experts, Mao planned to industrialise through small-scale production and the energy of the peasants in the new communes. For example, Mao encouraged the communes to establish backyard blast furnaces to produce steel.

Timeline

Chinese economy, 1958–62

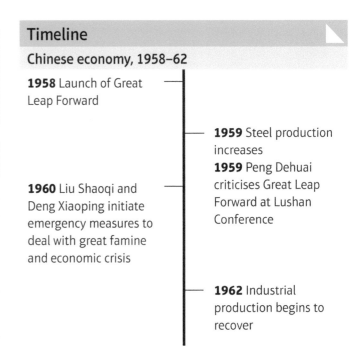

1958 Launch of Great Leap Forward

1959 Steel production increases

1959 Peng Dehuai criticises Great Leap Forward at Lushan Conference

1960 Liu Shaoqi and Deng Xiaoping initiate emergency measures to deal with great famine and economic crisis

1962 Industrial production begins to recover

Successes of the Great Leap Forward

The campaign succeeded in gaining the enthusiastic support of the peasants. As many as 90 million peasants were involved in building furnaces and producing steel in the first year of the Great Leap Forward.

There were also some successes in the modernisation of farms. In 1958, the amount of farmland that benefited from irrigation doubled. Also, the workforce of factories doubled between 1957 and 1960.

By the end of 1958, almost half of China's steel output was being produced by small-scale furnaces. Mao proclaimed the policy a success. What is more, in the early phase of the programme, it was a political success: Mao seemed to have developed a distinctively Chinese method of industrialisation, superior to the Soviet method of Five-Year Plans. The apparent success of the Great Leap Forward was highlighted in reports from each commune, stressing the rate and quantity of production.

The Lushan Conference, 1959

The Lushan Conference took place in July 1959, almost a year after the launch of the Great Leap Forward. The conference was an opportunity for senior communists to review the progress of the new policy.

Peng Dehuai, one of Mao's oldest allies, attended the conference. Peng was widely respected as a military leader who had played a key role in defeating the GMD during the Civil War. Prior to the conference, Peng had visited a commune. He had seen the beginnings of the famine and the huge waste of resources that the backyard furnace policy was creating.

Peng raised the problems of the policy with Mao in a private letter (see page 54), to avoid criticising the policy. Even so, Mao took Peng's letter as an attack, and therefore publicly denounced and sacked Peng.

Source C

A government photograph of Peng Dehuai taken in 1959.

The importance of the conference

The Lushan Conference was extremely significant in terms of the failure of the second Five-Year Plan and the Great Leap Forward. In essence, Mao used the conference to persecute critics of the policy and therefore suppress the truth of the crisis that was developing in China.

The conference demonstrated that Mao was not prepared to tolerate criticism, and that any criticism would lead to humiliation or even the arrest of the critics. Therefore, the conference had the following consequences:

- It led Mao to launch an 'Anti-Right Opportunist Campaign', which persecuted Party members who dared to criticise the Great Leap Forward. He accused them of 'rightist opportunism' – going against CCP policy and the communes. Many critics were sent to labour camps.
- It persuaded senior Party members to continue lying about the chaos caused by the Great Leap Forward.
- It delayed recognition that the Great Leap Forward was creating huge economic problems, and therefore delayed the adoption of new policies to deal with the growing famine.
- It led Mao to advocate a 'second Leap', in which the disastrous policies of the Great Leap Forward were expanded. For example, targets for steel production were increased, making the crisis worse.

Interpretation 3

From *Party vs. State in Post-1949 China* by Shiping Zheng, published in 1997.

However, the policy dispute at the Lushan Conference in July prompted ... a new mass mobilisation ... People's communes were further expanded, and more public mess halls [canteens] were opened. The so-called wind of Communism was now sweeping through the rural areas. In industrial sectors, scarce resources, manpower, and machine tools were all pulled together in concerted efforts to reach the goals for iron and steel output. Hence, from late 1959 to the first half of 1960, the whole country underwent a second upsurge of the Great Leap Forward ... following the Lushan Conference.

Activity ?

Read Interpretation 3.

1 Summarise Interpretation 3's view of the main impact of the Lushan Conference.

2 List two other impacts of the Lushan Conference.

3 Categorise the impacts that you have identified from Interpretation 3 and your own knowledge.

4 Write a sentence explaining which of the impacts was the most important and why.

Failures of the Great Leap Forward

In reality, the Great Leap Forward was a disastrous policy which seriously damaged the economy.

Overall, heavy industrial production dropped by around 55% between 1959 and 1962, and the production of light industry declined by about 30% in the same period.

Additionally, the economic chaos meant that the government was forced to shut down factories that had been opened during the first Five-Year Plan. Indeed, 25,000 state enterprises were closed. New construction projects were also cancelled. As a result, around 8.5 million urban workers lost their jobs and were forced to leave the cities and find work in the country. In total, around 45% of industrial workers lost their jobs.

Industrial production, 1958–62			
Industry	Output, 1958 (million metric tons, mmt)	Output, 1960 (mmt)	Output, 1962 (mmt)
Steel	9	19	9
Coal	270	130	220
Cement	9.30	15.65	6.00

Reasons for failures

The Great Leap Forward failed for a number of reasons.

- Backyard furnaces destroyed useful tools and wasted labour. Peasants complied with Mao's orders to produce steel by melting down their pots and pans. The peasants destroyed their possessions enthusiastically, apparently believing that Mao's polices meant they would soon have better tools and kitchen implements. However, the quality of the steel produced was so poor that it could not be used.

- Equally, peasants heated their backyard furnaces by burning wooden furniture, rice bowls and wooden tools, as these were a readily available source of fuel. Again, this destroyed a great deal of wealth, in order to produce steel which had no value.

- In order to produce this steel, peasants diverted their efforts away from farming. This is one reason why agricultural production slumped, and was one of the causes of the great famine.

- Another reason for the failure of the campaign was false reporting. Local Party officials were put under enormous pressure to produce more steel, more grain, and to report good news. What is more, following the 'Anti-Rightist' purge (see page 36), they were scared to criticise government policy or to appear to be failing. Therefore, Party officials falsified their reports – they forged statistics – and refused to report problems with the policy. Senior figures were unable to spot problems and fix them for the first year of the campaign.

Source D

A photograph of peasants collecting metal tools to melt down in their commune's backyard furnace. The photo was taken in 1959.

Activities ?

1 In groups, discuss the early successes of the Great Leap Forward. Choose the one you think is the most significant and write a slogan for it, using no more than seven words.

2 Write a short three-act play about the Lushan Conference.

- Act 1 should feature Peng travelling to a commune and talking to peasants about their problems.

- Act 2 should feature the audience reacting to Mao's speech and sacking Peng at the Lushan Conference.

- Act 3 should feature senior Party leaders reacting to news that Mao has launched the 'Anti-Right Opportunist Campaign'.

3 Imagine you are Mao. Write an entry in your diary listing three reasons why you ignored the advice of Peng Dehuai.

Economic reform, 1962–65

From 1960, CCP leaders were forced to acknowledge the scale of the economic crisis and the hardship caused by the great famine, which became known as the Three Bad Years. At the time of the Lushan Conference, Mao had assumed that Peng was lying about China's problems in order to take over the leadership of the government. However, by the end of 1959, Mao realised that his policy had failed.

Mao responded to the crisis by retiring from the centre of government. Apparently, Mao temporarily lost faith in the future of Chinese communism. During June–November 1960, Liu Shaoqi and Deng Xiaoping introduced a series of pragmatic reform policies to combat the famine and to reverse economic decline, including the restoration of private farming (see page 58). Mao remained chairman of the Party, and kept his official titles, but he allowed Liu and Deng to make the key decisions about how to solve the problems created by the Great Leap Forward.

In 1962, the pace of this reform was increased.

Reasons for reform

Liu and Deng's new economic policies were introduced for a series of reasons.

Mao's withdrawal from government

In 1960, Mao withdrew from the government. He did not leave politics entirely, but his authority at the top of government was seriously harmed by the failure of his policies. This allowed Liu and Deng to take control of economic policy.

Pragmatism

Liu and Deng were willing to abandon the utopian policies of the Great Leap Forward and introduce more pragmatic policies, such as the restoration of private farming (see page 59). Deng famously defended pragmatism with a metaphor about cats and mice. In 1962 he argued: 'Whether white or black, a cat is a good cat so long as it catches the rat.' Deng's point was that economic policies should be judged on their results. The Great Leap Forward appeared ideologically correct but it had failed. Therefore, it was time to try a new policy that was less radical and utopian, but stood a better chance of working in the longer term.

The decline in popular support

Famine had changed public opinion in China. The popular enthusiasm that had accompanied the Great Leap Forward had disappeared. Overall, the people were disillusioned with utopian projects. Throughout China, people wanted an end to famine, and improvements in living standards. Therefore, they supported policies that emphasised hard work and higher pay, rather than utopian enthusiasm.

Restoring control

The famine had led to a breakdown in political control across some areas of the country. As the communes failed, some peasants joined gangs of bandits who robbed and terrorised other peasants. Loss of government control was a particular problem in Sichuan and Tibet. The government introduced new policies to regain control.

Source E

A government poster created in 1960 by the CCP. The text says 'Getting organised is boundlessly good'.

Activity

Study Source C on page 69, Source B on page 68 and Source E on this page.

1 Write three bullet points describing the themes of posters promoting the Great Leap Forward and collectivisation. Link each bullet point to a detail from a source.

2 Write three bullet points describing the themes of Source E promoting Liu and Deng's reforms. Link each bullet point to a detail from the source.

3 Write a paragraph describing the differences between the themes of Source E and the previous posters.

Features of economic reform, 1962–65

Liu and Deng's policies were designed to end the great famine and to solve the problems that had been created by the Great Leap Forward.

Expertise

First, Liu and Deng employed economic planners and experts, who had been dismissed during the 'Anti-Rightist' purge (see page 37). During the great famine, experts had devised a system of rationing to solve the problem of food distribution.

Experts were also important in terms of rice production. In 1962, Liu and Deng instructed the Chinese Academy of Agricultural Sciences to develop a new strain of rice to boost production. The result, dwarf rice, produced around one-third more than traditional rice varieties. Dwarf rice was introduced across China in 1964.

The employment of experts was a significant change in policy as, during the Great Leap Forward, Mao had stressed the need for mass mobilisation rather than expert authority.

Incentives

The payment system was reformed, so that people were rewarded for hard work. Bonuses and prizes were introduced as an extra incentive to boost production. As part of this reform, managers were told to emphasise discipline on farms and in factories, rather than ideology. In the countryside, the restoration of private farming (see page 59) also created incentives by allowing peasants to sell some of their crops to make a profit.

Industrial reform

In order to use resources efficiently, Liu and Deng ordered the closure of thousands of small factories and workshops. Backyard furnaces were also phased out. Hierarchical management structures* were put in place to ensure that experts were in control of factories. Finally, targets for industrial growth were lowered, which made them more achievable and led to fewer attempts to distort production figures.

Key term

Hierarchical management structures*

A system of organisation in which leaders have a great deal of power over the people they lead.

The consequences of economic reform

Liu and Deng's reforms helped the economy to recover. However, they also had political consequences, which caused problems for the government.

Economic consequences

By the end of 1962, the economy had stabilised. From 1962 to 1965, industry grew at a rate of 11% a year. However, this was achieved, in part, by sacking large numbers of industrial workers in order to make factories more efficient. A 'return to the village' campaign, which encouraged workers to return to farming, led to a 50% drop in the industrial workforce.

Farming, too, began to recover from 1962. Grain production rose from 147.5 million tons in 1961 to 214.0 million tons in 1966.

Source F

From an article published in November 1962 in the *Peking Review*. This was the weekly magazine of Chinese news published by the CCP.

China's young petroleum industry is growing fast. Output is rising. In the first eight months of this year, the output of gasoline, kerosene and lubricating oil increased from 28 per cent to over 100 per cent, compared with the same period last year.

Like other branches of industry the oil industry is making its contribution to the nationwide drive to aid agriculture. An increasing amount of oil for farm machinery, pumping and irrigation works had been sent to the countryside.

Source G

From an oral history of the great famine published in 2013. Here a woman called Xian looks back at her experience as a 12-year-old student in a music school in 1962.

It was in 1962 that I first experienced real hunger. ... I remember that at the time the canteen used to have a big wok lying on the ground that contained a dark-coloured sweet potato soup. We were told that the heavy rain had killed large quantities of crops in the countryside.

The state had no free food to give away. The only food these villagers had kept in reserve were rotten sweet potatoes.

One of my classmates ... had relatives who lived abroad. They sent her some food ... But she didn't dare to touch the food.

Political consequences

Liu and Deng's policies created political problems. Specifically, the reforms in agriculture and industry led to a re-emergence of inequality. The biggest sign of inequality was between peasants and workers. In the cities, workers increasingly had consumer goods, such as watches, radios, sewing machines and bicycles, which the vast majority of peasants could not afford.

Exam-style question, Section B

Study Sources F and G.

How useful are Sources F and G for an enquiry into the strength of the Chinese economy in 1962?

Explain your answer, using Sources F and G and your knowledge of the historical context. **8 marks**

Exam tip

When considering how useful sources are, be sure to focus on the subject of the enquiry. Consider the information the sources provide and think about how the purpose of the source might affect its usefulness. Don't forget to consider the historical context.

There were inequalities in the countryside, too. Lucky or hardworking peasants grew wealthy due to their ability to farm their own land and trade. Liu and Deng's critics argued that the reforms helped create a new class of wealthy and powerful experts. This was against the spirit of Maoism, and supporters of Mao grew suspicious that Liu and Deng were no longer following truly communist policies.

Summary

- Mao introduced the second Five-Year Plan, the Great Leap Forward, in 1958. It was part of a radicalisation of economic policy.
- The Great Leap Forward was an attempt to increase industrial and agricultural production through the mass mobilisation of Chinese peasants.
- The Great Leap Forward failed to meet Mao's aims.
- Peng Dehuai highlighted problems with Mao's policy at the Lushan Conference in 1959.
- Mao rejected criticism and initiated a 'second Leap'.
- Liu Shaoqi and Deng Xiaoping introduced pragmatic policies to help the economy recover.

Checkpoint

Strengthen

S1 Describe two features of the Great Leap Forward.

S2 Give two examples of the failure of the Great Leap Forward.

S3 Outline the different stages of Chinese economic policy between 1949 and 1965.

Challenge

C1 Explain why the Great Leap Forward failed to meet Mao's aims.

C2 Write a paragraph explaining how far you believe Liu and Deng's policies led to the recovery of the Chinese economy by 1965.

C3 Write a paragraph giving your view on how far the CCP's economic policy succeeded in the years 1949–65.

If you can't answer these questions in the form of a paragraph, try writing down the pieces of information that you can recall on a large sheet of paper. Draw lines between them to show the relationships between the different pieces of information. You could do this in pairs or in small groups. Use this as a plan as a basis for your paragraph.

Recap: Economic policy, 1949–65

Recall quiz

1 List the different types of farm introduced by the CCP in the years 1949–57.

2 What was the difference between the Advanced APCs and the communes?

3 List three key features of a commune.

4 Explain why Mao introduced the communes.

5 When was the Lushan Conference?

6 List three consequences of the Lushan Conference.

7 Give three reasons why Mao introduced the first Five-Year Plan in 1953.

8 Which area of the economy grew most during the first Five-Year Plan?

9 Give three reasons why Mao introduced the Great Leap Forward.

10 Explain how pragmatism is different from utopianism.

Activity ?

Copy and complete the following table to indicate the key changes that took place in China in the years 1949–65.

In 1949	In 1965
The Chinese farms were …	The Chinese farms were …
The CCP controlled …	The CCP controlled …
The problems affecting people in urban areas included …	The problems affecting people in urban areas included …
The majority of farms were owned by …	The majority of farms were owned by …
The majority of factories were owned by …	The majority of factories were owned by …

In the exam, you will be asked how useful sources are for an enquiry. Copy and complete the following table. Support what you say with your own knowledge if it helps you to make your point.

Source	Enquiry	Ways they are useful
B (page 44) and C (page 45)	The impact of land reform	
C (page 51) and D (page 52)	The impact of the communes	
F and G (page 54)	The success of the communes	
A (page 62) and B (page 63)	The reason for the introduction of the first Five-Year Plan	
D (page 64) and E (page 65)	The success of the first Five-Year Plan	
F and G (page 73)	The strength of the Chinese economy in 1962	

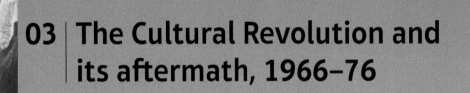

03 | The Cultural Revolution and its aftermath, 1966–76

The Cultural Revolution was one of the most violent and chaotic episodes in Mao's rule. For two years, urban areas were terrorised by groups of Red Guards, who Mao encouraged to rebel against pragmatists in the CCP and academics, experts and managers.

The Red Guards attacked symbols of the 'old' China, such as religion and culture. They also attacked symbols of the 'old' capitalist world, such as women who wore Western styles. Mao believed that traditional culture and traditional ways of thinking were an obstacle to the creation of a truly socialist China.

The Cultural Revolution served an important political purpose: it eliminated Mao's rivals from the CCP and from government. Mao's prime rivals, Liu Shaoqi and Deng Xiaoping, were purged, allowing Mao to regain control.

However, the Cultural Revolution created problems for Mao. Firstly, having encouraged students to rebel, Mao had to find a way to bring the revolution to an end. Secondly, new factions and new disputes emerged in the CCP.

By the end of 1976, a decade after it began, the Cultural Revolution finally came to an end. However, its consequences lived on. For many of China's students who had been part of the revolution, the period was a lost decade.

Learning outcomes

In this chapter, you will find out about:

- Mao's political and ideological reasons for launching the Cultural Revolution
- how the Red Guards terrorised the CCP and the government
- what happened to Chinese politics, society and the economy as a result of the Cultural Revolution
- how Mao and Zhou Enlai dealt with the consequences of the Cultural Revolution.

3.1 Reasons for the Cultural Revolution

Learning outcomes

- Understand the reasons for the struggle for power.
- Understand Mao's goal of purifying communism.

Mao was primarily responsible for initiating the Cultural Revolution. He had two main motives.

- **Political reasons:** Mao wanted to regain control of the CCP from Liu Shaoqi and Deng Xiaoping.
- **Ideological reasons:** Mao believed that the CCP had lost its revolutionary spirit and that there was a danger of a return to capitalism in China.

The power struggle

Mao launched the Cultural Revolution as part of a struggle to regain control of the CCP. Following the failures of the Great Leap Forward, Mao had delegated the task of ending the famine and reviving the economy to Liu Shaoqi and Deng Xiaoping, and had withdrawn from the centre of government. While he continued as chairman of the CCP, and was involved in some government work, he handed over the presidency of the PRC to Liu.

Initially, Mao allowed Liu and Deng to play the main role. However, by 1962, Mao believed that Liu and Deng were going too far. Mao was critical of their emphasis on private farming, and on expert management of industry. Mao also felt snubbed by Liu and Deng, who increasingly ran government without consulting him.

Mao's authority

Mao was particularly concerned about his loss of authority at the top of government. While the majority of the population still respected Mao, senior officials trusted Liu and Deng because their policies had ended the famine and were creating economic growth.

Mao's loss of authority became obvious during the early 1960s, when he struggled to persuade the government to implement his ideas. Between 1962 and 1964, Mao tried to launch five new initiatives, to:

- stop the growth of private farming
- reform the school and university curriculum
- increase investment in rural healthcare
- create an organisation to allow peasants to challenge the authority of the CCP
- begin cultural reform in order to stamp out traditional ideas.

Liu and Deng refused to implement Mao's ideas. In response, Mao began to plot his return to power.

Source A

A photograph of Mao Zedong in 1961 in the Chinese countryside, taken by a CCP photographer.

The purification of communism

The Cultural Revolution was also designed to regain control of the CCP. Mao wanted to purify communism by removing the influence of capitalism. Mao was concerned about the policies of Liu and Deng:

- the break-up of communes
- the reintroduction of private farming
- the introduction of incentives in industry and agriculture
- the growth of bureaucracy
- the increasing importance of experts in economic planning and industrial production.

The 'capitalist road'

For Mao, these policies showed that Liu and Deng had taken the 'capitalist road' (see Figure 3.1). Experts had grown wealthy and powerful, and Mao was worried that the government was ignoring workers and peasants. He was determined to preserve the spirit of the revolution and end the domination of the pragmatists.

Mao was so concerned that, from the mid-1960s, he warned that the biggest danger threatening communist rule in China was revisionism* by what he called 'capitalist roaders'*.

Key terms

Revisionism*

A term used by Mao and his followers to describe ideas and policies that undermined socialism. For example, Mao argued that the reintroduction of private farming was an example of revisionism. Mao argued that it changed, or revised, the initial socialist policy of communes in which everything belonged to the state.

'Capitalist roaders'*

Mao and his allies used the term 'capitalist roaders' to describe members of the CCP who favoured 'revisionist' policies. Mao argued that they had effectively decided to take the 'capitalist road'.

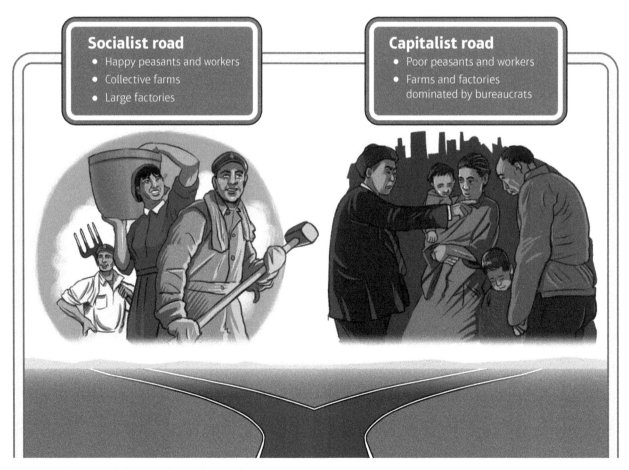

Figure 3.1 Mao's view of the socialist and capitalist roads.

Source B

From an interview with a junior CCP official given in 1980. The interviewee worked as a translator for the government in Beijing from 1964.

> We were several hundred in the bureau, which was headed by a director and two deputy directors. They were cadres [officials] of high status ... The director had a chauffeur-driven car and the high rank of a deputy minister ... His rank entitled him to a beautiful old Peking-style four-corner courtyard house ... with an inner garden complete with fruit trees. He had his own private telephone and his home was well furnished, with deep soft sofas and armchairs, rugs, even a refrigerator.

> **Exam-style question, Section A**
>
> Give **two** things you can infer from Source B about the privileges of members of the CCP before the Cultural Revolution.
>
> **4 marks**

> **Exam tip**
>
> You infer something from a source by working out something the source does not actually tell you directly. Make sure you support the inference using details from the source.

Reform of education

Mao believed that educational reforms introduced after 1960 were further evidence that the CCP was following the wrong road. In 1960, education minister Yang Xiu-feng had set out a new system of schooling, designed to be more modern and efficient than the traditional system.

- Yang was keen to ensure that students studied the most modern science and technology. Yang argued that this focus on science was essential to producing a new generation of technicians and experts to work in industry.
- Yang also introduced a system in which the children of CCP members went to the best schools, whereas other children attended schools with fewer resources, larger class sizes and a narrower range of subjects.

Mao argued that Yang's reforms reflected the wrong values. Mao rejected Yang's emphasis on the need for experts and his emphasis on science. Rather, Mao argued that education should serve the masses and focus on ideology. Secondly, Mao believed that Yang's reforms gave special privileges to the CCP. Mao rejected this, arguing for an egalitarian* education system in which all children were treated equally.

> **Key term**
>
> **Egalitarian***
> Equal, based on the principle that people should be treated equally.

Mao's allies

In the run-up to the Cultural Revolution, Mao relied on his allies, Lin Biao and Jiang Qing, to help him achieve his goal of purifying communism.

Lin Biao

Lin Biao was Mao's most influential ally. He was China's defence minister and head of the PLA, and was a devoted supporter of Mao. Mao worked closely with Lin for a number of reasons:

- He believed that Lin and the PLA had retained a pure revolutionary spirit.
- The PLA was a powerful organisation which could help Mao regain power.
- Lin had produced a pocket-sized book, *Quotations from Chairman Mao Tse-tung*, known as the 'Little Red Book', which was given to every Chinese soldier. Lin insisted that the PLA should study Mao's words.

Source C

A photograph of some PLA soldiers reading *Quotations from Chairman Mao Tse-tung*, the 'Little Red Book'. The photograph was taken by a PLA photographer during the Cultural Revolution.

Jiang Qing

Mao wanted to revive the revolutionary spirit throughout China. He also hoped that regaining power would be part of a broader cultural revolution. Therefore, he needed the help of intellectuals, people who understood culture and propaganda. Mao's leading intellectual ally in purifying communism was Jiang Qing, his wife, who had important contacts in the propaganda department in Shanghai. Jiang was also interested in reforming culture, particularly opera and ballet.

Activities

1. In one sentence, describe why Mao wanted to purify communism in China.
2. Draw a diagram to show Mao, his allies and his opponents in 1966. Make sure you list the key strengths and positions of power held by Mao and his allies, as well as by his opponents.
3. With a partner, write one paragraph arguing why Liu and Deng's policies benefited the Chinese people and one paragraph arguing why the policies did not benefit them.

Extend your knowledge

Lin Biao

Lin Biao was a hero of the Civil War, and of China's war with Japan during the Second World War. Indeed, Lin's work as a military leader played a key role in a number of important victories.

Lin replaced Peng Dehuai as defence minister and leader of the PLA in 1959. Lin's emphasis on the teachings of Mao, and on removing Soviet influence from the PLA, pleased Mao. Lin played a key role in the Cultural Revolution. However, Mao grew increasingly suspicious of his former ally. Lin died in controversial circumstances in 1971 (see page 96), and was later blamed for the chaos and terror of the Cultural Revolution.

Extend your knowledge

Jiang Qing

Jiang Qing spent her early life as an actress in Shanghai. She became Mao's fourth wife in 1938. Jiang was an intellectual, and worked as Mao's personal assistant before leading the CCP's Propaganda Film Department in the 1950s. She was interested in culture and was a committed Maoist. Additionally, she was well connected to radical intellectuals in Shanghai. She was an obvious choice to play a leading role in the Cultural Revolution.

Jiang was a shrewd politician and used the Cultural Revolution to destroy her own enemies and rivals. She was also ambitious and wanted to play a key role in government after Mao's death.

However, following Mao's death, she was soon arrested. Jiang was sentenced to death in 1981, but her punishment was changed to a life sentence. She was released due to ill-health in 1991 and later committed suicide.

Source D

A photograph of Jiang Qing. The photograph was taken by a Chinese press photographer during the Cultural Revolution.

The Socialist Education Movement

The Socialist Education Movement, developed in 1962, was one of Mao's first attempts to reassert his authority in the CCP. The campaign was designed to re-educate Party members, in order to stamp out revisionism. Mao's ten points launched the campaign nationally in 1963. They set out his aims that the Socialist Education Movement would:

- expand collectivisation in farming
- purify the CCP by ending the privileged status of Party members
- ensure that the CCP trusted peasants and workers rather than experts.

Mao hoped that the Socialist Education Movement would become a mass campaign, like the 'antis' movements. Indeed, Mao wanted to encourage workers and peasants to purge the party of revisionists and 'capitalist roaders'. However, Liu and Deng issued instructions that the new campaign should be controlled by the CCP, not by the people. Therefore, the Socialist Education Movement failed to achieve Mao's aim of purifying the CCP, because CCP officials ensured that the campaign did not challenge their power.

Source E

From an article in the *People's Daily*, published on 1 January 1964.

```
The movement of socialist education ... is a
great revolutionary movement of re-educating
the people in proletarian, socialist ideology
and uniting ... the mass of the people to
struggle against class enemies ...

In the new year, the socialist education
movement should be carried forward ... Cadres
[members of the CCP] at all levels should take
part in this movement ... While helping with
the work at a basic level, they should draw
upon lessons together with the masses and
thereby help raise their own political level.
```

Interpretation 1

From *China's Unfinished Revolution* by Dennis M. Ray, published in 1970.

The Socialist Education Movement attempted to reaffirm Mao's hard class line by attacking revisionism ... Not all within the Chinese Communist oligarchy, however, looked upon revisionism with the same horror ... As Mao attempted to reverse the revisionism of China through incessant class struggle, he became disillusioned with his lifelong comrades who seemed less than enthusiastic.

Campaign against capitalist culture

In 1965, Mao initiated a campaign against capitalist culture. He instructed his allies to criticise the play *Hai Rui dismissed from office*. The play was written by Wu Nan about a 16th-century government official who had been persecuted for criticising the Chinese emperor. Wu Nan was an important writer. He was vice-mayor of Beijing, and a supporter of Liu and Deng. Mao's allies argued that his play was an allegory for Peng Dehuai's persecution after he criticised Mao's Great Leap Forward. Indeed, they argued that the play was anti-Maoist and therefore an example of the capitalist culture that was growing in China in the mid-1960s.

Jiang Qing arranged for articles criticising the play to be published in a Shanghai newspaper. The articles were the first step towards a broader criticism of culture under Liu and Deng.

Source F

A propaganda poster issued by the Cultural Revolution Group in 1967. The text reads 'Proletarian revolutionaries unite under the great red banner of the thoughts of Mao Zedong!'

Source G

From an article in the *Opera Battle News*, published during the Cultural Revolution. The Opera Battle News was a magazine published by radical communists.

In this moment when the dark cloud was rolling up, our beloved Comrade Jiang Qing raised high the mighty banner of Mao Zedong Thought, planting it firmly in the field of literature, and gave battle to the ox-demons and snake-specters. After Comrade Jiang Qing had seen *Hai Rui [Hai Jui]* ... With one glance she perceived the political conspiracy hidden in *Hai Rui [Hai Jui]* ... and instantly gave the ... directive: 'This is a bad play; stop performances.'

THINKING HISTORICALLY ▷ Cause and consequence (2b)

Events and conditions

Study the living graph below, which shows the importance of the causes that led to the introduction of the Great Leap Forward.

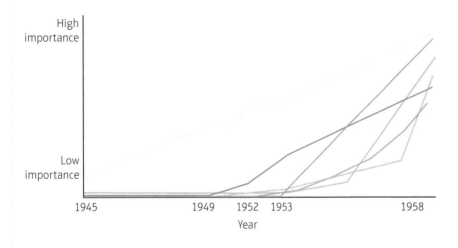

Key
- Conflict with the USSR
- Success of the first Five-Year Plan
- Mao's ideology
- Mao's prestige
- Need to industrialise
- Success of collectivisation

Make your own living graph for the Cultural Revolution, using the following causes.

The power struggle	Mao's alliances	Controversy over Wu Nan's play
Mao's ideology	Liu and Deng's policies	The failure of the Socialist Education Movement

1 Which of the causes would you describe as '**conditions**' and which would you describe as '**triggers**'? Explain your answer. Are there any that don't fit either term?

2 Which of the causes would you describe as 'long-term' and which would you describe as 'short-term'?

3 How does knowing the different levels of importance that the causes had at different times help you to explain why an event happened?

The Twenty-Three Articles

In January 1965, Mao published the Twenty-Three Articles, setting out his strategy for purging the CCP. He proposed that workers and peasants should be allowed to form groups and attack corrupt officials. However, Liu Shaoqi refused to allow the formation of these groups, as he feared attacks on officials would damage the economy.

The Central Cultural Revolution Group

Following criticism of Wu Nan's play, the CCP set up a committee called the Five Man Group in order to purge Chinese culture. The committee was led by Peng Zhen, an ally of Liu and Deng Xiaoping. Indeed, Liu and Deng hoped to keep control of the group in order to stop it destabilising their power.

The Five Man Group refused to condemn Wu Nan's opera. Therefore, in May 1966, Mao dismissed the Five Man Group and founded the Cultural Revolution Group to oversee a true purge of Chinese culture. The new group was full of Mao's allies and was led by Jiang Qing. Jiang and the Cultural Revolution Group quickly took control of the CCP's propaganda department, removing supporters of Liu and Deng. Jiang used government propaganda to appeal to young people to join a new movement, called the Red Guards, to help purge the CCP of 'capitalist roaders'.

Launching the Cultural Revolution

Initially, Liu and Deng supported Mao's new campaign against capitalist culture. Indeed, they supported a resolution by the Politburo in May 1966 to initiate a Cultural Revolution. It seems that Liu and Deng hoped to keep control of the Cultural Revolution, as they had kept control of the Socialist Education Movement. However, Mao and his allies were better prepared. As a result, Liu and Deng were unable to control the new campaign, which quickly created chaos across the whole country.

Activities

1 Make a flow chart of the factors leading to the launch of the Cultural Revolution.

2 Imagine you are working for Jiang Qing. Write a newspaper headline denouncing *Hai Jui dismissed from office*. Underneath, list the three main points you would want to make in the article.

3 Imagine you are advising Mao. List the points you would suggest he makes in a speech to launch the Cultural Revolution.

Summary

- Following the failure of the Great Leap Forward, Mao became convinced that the CCP was abandoning socialism.
- During the early 1960s, Mao believed that Liu and Deng had taken control of government away from him.
- Mao tried to revive his authority within the government through the Socialist Education Movement, but Liu and Deng prevented this by taking control of the campaign.
- Mao and his allies launched the Cultural Revolution after criticising Wu Nan in 1965.

Checkpoint

Strengthen

S1 Describe the differences between Mao's vision of socialism and the policies of Liu and Deng.

S2 Explain the reasons why Mao criticised Yang's educational reforms.

S3 Explain the meaning of 'revisionism'.

Challenge

C1 In your own words, summarise Mao's reasons for working with Lin Biao.

C2 'Mao's main aim in launching the Cultural Revolution was to purify communism.' How far do you agree?

If you can't answer these questions, look through this chapter for key words and re-read those sections.

3.2 The Red Guards and the Red Terror

The Great Proletarian Cultural Revolution was designed to revitalise communism and reassert Mao's control of China. However, it led to chaos, mass terror, millions of deaths and an intense power struggle inside the CCP.

The most chaotic period of the Cultural Revolution took place between August 1966 and April 1969, a period of Red Terror. During this time, the newly formed Red Guards persecuted members of the CCP, industrial managers, academics and even other factions* of Red Guards.

By April 1969, Mao had eliminated his opponents.

Key term

Factions*

Groups within a larger group.

Mao's hold on young people

During the first phase of the Cultural Revolution, Mao appealed to students and young people. Students responded by forming groups of Red Guards and rebelling against their teachers and lecturers.

Mao and Jiang assumed that the majority of students and young people would support the struggle against Liu and Deng. Students and young people had been hard hit by education reforms under Liu and Deng (see 'Student grievances', page 85). Therefore, students would be eager for radical change.

In January 1966, the CCP began mass producing *Quotations from Chairman Mao Tse-tung* and issuing it to students. The 'Little Red Book', as it became known, encouraged students to rebel against CCP authority.

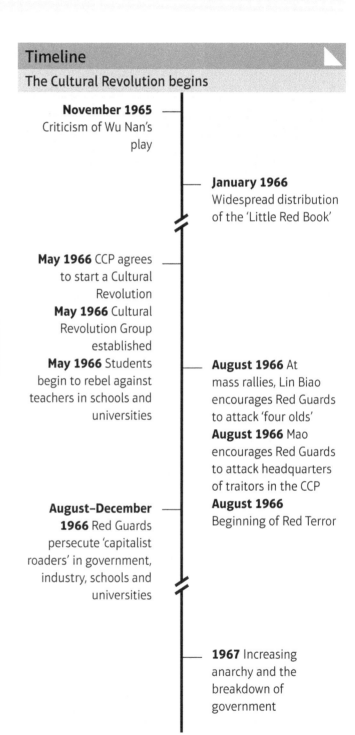

Timeline
The Cultural Revolution begins

November 1965
Criticism of Wu Nan's play

January 1966
Widespread distribution of the 'Little Red Book'

May 1966 CCP agrees to start a Cultural Revolution
May 1966 Cultural Revolution Group established
May 1966 Students begin to rebel against teachers in schools and universities

August 1966 At mass rallies, Lin Biao encourages Red Guards to attack 'four olds'
August 1966 Mao encourages Red Guards to attack headquarters of traitors in the CCP
August 1966 Beginning of Red Terror

August–December 1966 Red Guards persecute 'capitalist roaders' in government, industry, schools and universities

1967 Increasing anarchy and the breakdown of government

Student grievances

Yang Xiu-feng's educational reforms had led to growing inequalities in education. The children of CCP officials were able to attend elite schools and get places at top universities. Many other young people, who were denied places at university, were sent to the countryside to do poorly-paid work on farms.

Yang's educational policies led to a great deal of resentment among young people, particularly in the cities (see Figure 3.2). As a result, young people were eager to join the Red Guards and fight the CCP elite.

The emergence of the Red Guards

In May 1966, inspired by reading the 'Little Red Book', students began to organise themselves into groups of Red Guards. The Red Guards were groups of students from China's universities and schools. Each group of Red Guards was organised like an army battalion, wearing a military-style uniform. The Red Guards were devoted to the teachings of Mao and attacked revisionists.

Attacks on universities

In May 1966, Beijing University students began protests against their university lecturers. In June, Red Guards in Beijing began physically attacking lecturers. Powerful people, such as industrial managers, were also attacked on the streets of Beijing. Mao praised the student rebels, assuring them that they had his support.

In August 1966, the CCP published the Sixteen Articles, which gave the new Red Guards the right to overthrow 'capitalist roaders', and people with old ideas. By August 1966, radical groups of Red Guards were running many of China's universities, having purged the universities of teachers and administrators.

Source A

From a speech by Mao Zedong about the role of teachers in China. The speech was given in 1965, but was published again at the beginning of the Cultural Revolution.

The next few decades will be precious and important for the future of our country and the destiny of mankind. The twenty-year-old will be forty or fifty in twenty or thirty years' time. This generation of young people will take part in building our poor and bare country into a great strong socialist power and will fight and bury imperialism with their own hands. The task is arduous and the road long. Chinese people of lofty ambitions must dedicate their lives to the accomplishment of our great historic mission ...

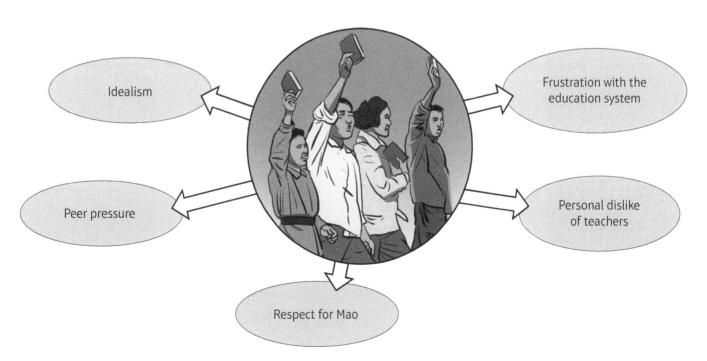

Figure 3.2 Reasons for student rebellion.

Idealism

Frustration with the education system

Peer pressure

Personal dislike of teachers

Respect for Mao

Source B

From the recollections of Ma Xiaodong, the daughter of a CCP official born in Beijing, published in 2005. Ma was in her early teens when the Cultural Revolution began.

I was disappointed that I didn't get into the school of my first choice, the prestigious Beijing Normal University's Affiliated Secondary School for Girls. ... I cried for a week when I learned that I was only admitted to my third and also last choice, the No. 8 Girls' Secondary School.

We also had the revolutionising movement in my school. Sometimes we had such long meetings that we ended up spending the night at school, sleeping on desks. I remember the two goals of the movement: to guard against ... [American Imperialism] and to continue the proletarian revolution.

Exam-style question, Section B

Study Sources A and B. How useful are the sources for an enquiry into the reasons why students joined the Red Guards at the beginning of the Cultural Revolution? Explain your answer, using Sources A and B and your knowledge of the historical context.

8 marks

Exam tip

When considering how useful sources are, be sure to focus on the subject of the enquiry. Consider the information the sources provide and think about how the origin of the source – who wrote it and when – might affect its usefulness.

Extend your knowledge

Mao and the Beijing Commune

Mao appealed to students to rise up and build a new form of government. He encouraged them to create democratic communes, which were free of the control of the CCP. The Beijing Commune was the first experiment in this kind of radical democratic organisation and was established at Beijing University in 1966. During the Cultural Revolution, democratic communes were established in other places, such as Shanghai. Mao eventually disbanded the new democratic communes as he could not control them.

Mass rallies

Between August and December, the Cultural Revolution escalated. Red Guards unleashed terror against Mao's enemies, attacking revisionists in major cities, and supporters of Liu and Deng inside the CCP. Mao played a key role in encouraging the Red Terror through speaking at mass rallies and issuing radical orders.

Between mid-August and November 1966, Mao's supporters organised eight massive rallies. They took place in Tiananmen Square, a location that was associated with rebellion, and the place where Mao had announced the formation of the PRC in 1949. Around 12 million Red Guards attended the rallies. Mao was celebrated as the 'great teacher' and 'great helmsman', and wore a red armband, the symbol of the Red Guards.

Mao and Lin Biao spoke at the rallies. The mass rallies had a significant impact on the Cultural Revolution. Millions of Red Guards heard Mao directly, and felt that they had been personally instructed to purge China of revisionists. They responded enthusiastically, chanting slogans such as 'It is justified to rebel', and 'Learn revolution by making revolution'. The rallies inspired millions of young people to rebel.

Source C

A photograph of Red Guards at a mass rally in Tiananmen Square in 1966. The photograph was taken by a Chinese press photographer.

Activity ?

In groups, discuss why Mao's instructions to rebel inspired so many young people. List at least three reasons why, in the context of the 1960s, young Chinese people were so keen to rebel.

Red Guard attacks on the 'four olds'

The mass rallies launched a campaign against the 'four olds'. Speaking at the rallies, Lin Biao encouraged the Red Guards to persecute anyone they believed:

- practised Old Customs
- respected Old Culture
- still had Old Habits
- believed Old Ideas.

In practice, Red Guards persecuted people who:

- read old or foreign books
- listened to foreign songs or sang traditional Chinese folk songs
- were dedicated to a religion.

Impact of the 'four olds' campaign

The 'four olds' campaign was a turning point in the Cultural Revolution. It encouraged the Red Guards to take their campaign outside of schools and universities. As a result, Red Guards took to the streets, terrorising anyone they suspected of old ways of behaving or thinking. This new phase in the Cultural Revolution was the beginning of a breakdown in order, as the Red Guards used terror against established authority across China.

Jiang Qing and the attack on the CCP

Mao also wanted to purge the CCP. Jiang played a key role in attacking the CCP. She used her control of the CCP's propaganda ministry to encourage the Red Guards to attack CCP officials.

Jiang also began publishing the names of high-level CCP officials, who she wanted the Red Guards to attack. Liu and Deng were named as the leaders of the 'capitalist roaders'. The Chinese media, controlled by the CCP, published articles detailing Liu and Deng's disloyalty to Mao, encouraging students to criticise Liu and Deng.

Red Guard attacks on the CCP

In August 1966, Mao issued one of his most radical orders. He personally put up a big character poster* instructing Red Guards to 'bombard the headquarters'. In essence, this was an instruction to storm the offices of the CCP, where Liu and Deng were based, and to terrorise CCP officials.

Key term

Big character poster*

Huge banners, which contain a slogan in big letters. Big character posters were traditionally used as a form of protest or propaganda. Big character posters played an important role in the development of the Cultural Revolution as Mao and his followers used them to communicate with the Red Guards.

Source D

A photograph of big character posters on a wall in Beijing. The photograph was originally published in a Chinese newspaper.

Source E

From the recollections of a Red Guard, published in 2009. He had been a student at Amoy University in Fujian province.

Between June and November 1966, we locked up almost every university ... professor, and lecturer. Every day we rounded them up and read them quotations from the works of Chairman Mao. ... Every day they had to clean the lavatories ... At night we made them write confessions 'asking Chairman Mao for punishment.' ... Once every three days we had a small struggle meeting, maybe with a few hundred persons, and once a week we mobilised a large struggle meeting with over a thousand people in attendance. That's when we really gave it to them.

Source F

From an article published by the Hsinhua News Agency on 22 August 1966. It describes events taking place in Beijing.

Launching a fierce offensive against all old ideas, culture, customs and habits, the 'Red Guards' in Peking ... have taken to the streets and have posted revolutionary handbills and big-character posters, held rallies and made speeches everywhere. ... they have proposed to the revolutionary staff and workers in the service trades that they never again give outlandish haircuts ... [or] sell ... decadent books or magazines. ... This rebel spirit and revolutionary action of the 'Red Guards' have won the most enthusiastic and resolute support of the broad masses of revolutionary teachers and students, revolutionary staff and workers and the city's residents.

Interpretation 1

From *A History of China* by Morris Rossabi, published in 2013.

The Red Guards attacked whatever smacked of the old society – monasteries, museums, and elaborate houses and courtyards. They then moved from destruction of objects to harassment of people. Members of the old elite and even Communist Party leaders were compelled to wear dunce caps [a sign of punishment] ... Even more destabilising were Red Guard and worker takeovers of universities, conservatories of music, and newspapers and magazines. They dismissed experts and sought to manage these institutions on their own, contributing to chaos in education and media outlets.

THINKING HISTORICALLY ▶ Evidence (2b&c)

Evidence and overall judgements

How violent were the Red Guards in the period late 1966? Study Sources E and F and Interpretation 1.

1 Which of the texts were written on the basis of personal experience of the events?

2 Which of the authors must have based their account(s) on studying evidence rather than on personal experience?

3 Is Source E or Source F more useful in helping us assess the level of violence of the Red Guards in late 1966?

4 Is there information in Interpretation 1 that people in 1966 probably didn't know? Explain your answer.

5 How do you think the author of Interpretation 1 got their information?

6 When thinking about the question of the extent of violence, does the historian have an advantage over an eyewitness? Explain your answer.

The growth of anarchy, 1967–68

During 1967 and 1968, the Cultural Revolution and the Red Terror grew. Attacks against revisionists and symbols of old philosophies increased. Consequently, government and industry began to break down and anarchy* increased.

The use of terror

The Red Guard's campaign against the 'four olds' and the CCP was extraordinarily violent, including beatings and killings. For example, they attacked:

- **People wearing Western clothes or with Western haircuts:** Red Guards forcibly cut the hair of women with braids or men with long hair. Women who wore dresses, skirts or high-heeled shoes had their clothes cut into pieces, and were forced to wear military uniforms.

- **Intellectuals, particularly teachers at universities:** many were forced to confess their crimes for hours in front of large crowds. Some were forced to march down streets wearing dunce's caps* and boards listing their crimes strapped to their chests. After being humiliated, some academics were sent to farms to be re-educated through study and hard labour. Others were forced to confess that they were monsters and demons. At Beijing University, some teachers were imprisoned in a local cowshed as punishment for their old ideas.

Key terms

Anarchy*

Disorder caused by lack of control by government.

Dunce's caps*

Tall, white, conical hats. Wearing a dunce's cap was a form of punishment or discipline for students.

Killings reached a height in 1968. Estimates suggest that between 1 and 2 million people were killed during the Cultural Revolution. The Red Terror affected the cities much more than rural areas. Around three-quarters of the killings took place in the cities. The government estimated that around 50% of the urban population were persecuted in some way by the Red Guards in the period 1966–68.

Activities

1. In groups, make a diagram of the factors leading to the growth of violence during the Cultural Revolution.

2. Discuss how useful Sources E and F are for an investigation into the causes of the growth of violence during the Cultural Revolution. Choose one strength and one limitation from each source.

3. How far do the sources support the view of Interpretation 1 about the extent of violence? Write a paragraph to explain your answer.

Source G

A photograph of a group of Red Guards taken by a Chinese press photographer in June 1966. The Red Guards shown in the photograph are high school and university students.

Exam-style question, Section A

Explain why Mao launched the Cultural Revolution in 1966.

You may use the following in your answer:

- Mao's ideology
- Liu Shaoqi.

You **must** also use information of your own.

12 marks

Exam tip

When answering a question like this, it is a good idea to discuss the bulleted points in your answer. However, to get the top marks you must also give information of your own to support your answer.

Cultural destruction

During 1967 and 1968, the Red Terror led to widespread cultural destruction.

- Works of art and books associated with old ideas were destroyed by Red Guards. Paintings were replaced by pictures of Mao and books were replaced by the works of Mao.
- Temples were ransacked and, in many cases, destroyed. Red Guards also demolished statues of Buddha and other religious relics (see also page 137).
- Red Guards broke into the homes of wealthy managers or CCP officials and destroyed their furniture, paintings and books. Western clothes were ripped to pieces or burned.

Source H

A poster from 1968. The poster was designed by the 'Bloody Bayonet' committee, a group of Red Guards based in Beijing. The text reads 'Whoever opposes Chairman Mao will have his dog head smashed in!'

The Red Guards also campaigned against old influences by changing the names of roads, parks and buildings. For example, the name of the Blue Sky Clothes Store was changed to Defend Mao Zedong Clothes Store, and Prosperity Street in central Beijing was renamed Anti-Revisionist Street.

Activity ?

In groups, decide how useful Sources E, F, G and H are for an enquiry into the significance of the Red Guards during the Cultural Revolution.

1. First, list aspects of the contents of the sources that are useful.
2. Second, list ways in which the sources are useful or limited based on their provenance.
3. Finally, write a paragraph stating which source is most useful and your reasons for this judgement.

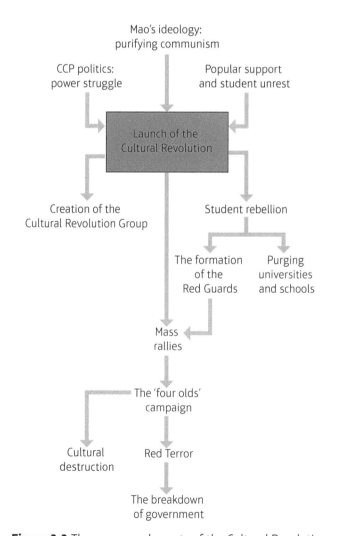

Figure 3.3 The causes and events of the Cultural Revolution.

Government breakdown

Mao aimed to use the Cultural Revolution to remove his enemies from government and create a new power base. However, by 1967 Red Guard violence was so extensive it led to the breakdown of government.

By early 1967, the Chinese government was facing a series of problems:

- The Cultural Revolution had spread across China. CCP officials were being attacked in all major cities.
- There was bitter fighting in the countryside between Red Guards, who were trying to stamp out private farming, and peasants, who wanted to keep control of their own land.
- There was street fighting in urban areas between Red Guards, who wanted to persecute factory managers, and workers, who wanted to keep production going to get their bonuses.
- The Red Guards were not united, and different factions fought each other on the streets.

The Red Guards took their rebellion further than Mao had intended, and this had undermined the government.

Summary

- Mao believed that students and young people would lead the campaign to reform Chinese culture and to end the power of his rivals in government.
- Jiang Qing used her influence over the Chinese media to attack the CCP and encourage the Red Guards to persecute Mao's enemies.
- The 'four olds' campaign led to further violence and the destruction of works of art and religious relics.
- By mid-1967, the Cultural Revolution had destroyed Mao's main rivals in the CCP but had led to anarchy across China.

Checkpoint

Strengthen

S1 Describe two features of the Red Guards.

S2 List three problems caused by the Cultural Revolution.

S3 Outline the different stages of the development of the Cultural Revolution from 1965 to 1968.

Challenge

C1 Explain why so many students joined the Red Guards.

C2 Summarise three ways in which the Red Guards helped remove Mao's enemies.

C3 List three consequences of the Cultural Revolution that Mao had not intended.

If you can't answer these questions, swap notes with someone in your group, and see if their notes can help you find the answer.

3.3 The effects of the Cultural Revolution

Learning outcomes

- Understand the political effects of the Cultural Revolution for the CCP.
- Understand the social effects of the Cultural Revolution for education.
- Understand the economic effects on industry and farming.

Timeline

Political effects, 1966–71

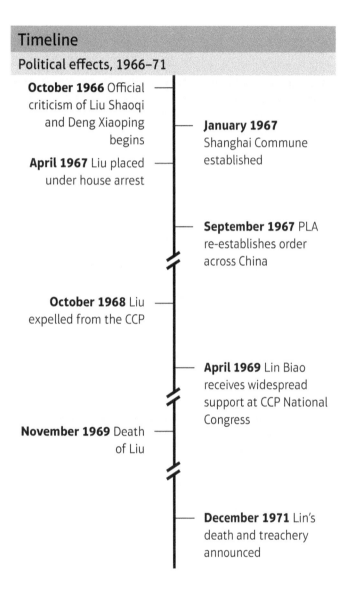

October 1966 Official criticism of Liu Shaoqi and Deng Xiaoping begins

January 1967 Shanghai Commune established

April 1967 Liu placed under house arrest

September 1967 PLA re-establishes order across China

October 1968 Liu expelled from the CCP

April 1969 Lin Biao receives widespread support at CCP National Congress

November 1969 Death of Liu

December 1971 Lin's death and treachery announced

The violence of the Cultural Revolution continued until 1971. Mao's final revolution had consequences far beyond anything that Mao had anticipated. In essence, the Cultural Revolution destroyed the power of Mao's rivals, but also led to political anarchy, chaos in education and major economic problems.

Political effects

Mao's re-emergence as the leader of China was the main political effect of the Cultural Revolution. Mao achieved this by purging Liu and Deng and other senior members of the CCP.

The purging of Liu Shaoqi and Deng Xiaoping

Mao quickly ended Liu and Deng's control of the CCP. Jiang Qing used her influence over the media to accuse them of supporting the 'capitalist road' and of being China's primary political enemies.

Source A

From 'Big Scab Liu Shao-chi', by Kung Hsiang-tung, an article published in 1969 in the *Peking Review*. The article attacked Liu Shaoqi. Kung was a leader of the CCP-dominated All-China Federation of Trade Unions.

During the last few decades, masquerading as the 'leader of the workers' movement', the big scab [a worker who betrays other workers] Liu Shao-chi engaged in deception and blackmail everywhere and committed innumerable crimes. He did his best to sell out the power of leadership of the working class ... In the crucial moments of the revolution, he brutally suppressed the workers' movement in a vain attempt to liquidate the proletarian revolution and subvert the proletarian dictatorship. He is a jackal ... He is the mortal foe of the working class.

Mao moved against Liu and Deng through a series of steps:

- Mao personally attacked Liu, calling him China's Khrushchev – implying that he was a bureaucrat, not a revolutionary.
- At the Eleventh Plenum, a high-level meeting of the CCP in August 1966, Liu was demoted.

- At a Party conference in October 1966, Liu and Deng were criticised for failing to support the Cultural Revolution and forced to engage in public self-criticism*.
- At the end of February 1967, Liu and Deng were publicly condemned as counter-revolutionaries and held responsible for the CCP's revisionist policies.
- During the summer of 1967, Liu was held under house arrest and repeatedly beaten. His son and wife were arrested and tortured. Deng was arrested and sent for re-education and hard labour on a farm.
- In October 1968, Liu was expelled from the CCP for being a traitor.
- Liu was kept under house arrest, starved, beaten, tortured and denied medical treatment until he died in November 1969.

Deng was later allowed to return to the government, but his powerbase had been destroyed.

Key term

Self-criticism*

A public confession of political mistakes. Self-criticism was often humiliating.

The purging of the CCP

According to the *People's Daily* newspaper, 28,000 CCP officials were arrested due to their association with Liu and Deng. As part of the purge of the leadership, about 70% of senior Party members were sent to labour camps for re-education. At lower levels of the Party, hundreds of thousands of officials were purged.

Many officials were sent to May 7th Cadre schools. These were large farms or camps where bureaucrats and intellectuals were re-educated on how to serve the people. There they had to undertake intensive political study of the works of Mao and Marx and engage in self-criticism, as well as work alongside the peasants, growing their own food.

The Shanghai Commune

The Red Guards did not stop once Liu and Deng had been purged from the government. Radical students wanted to go further and challenge the authority of the CCP throughout the country.

The Shanghai Commune, established in January 1967, is one example of the radical purge of the CCP which happened during the Cultural Revolution. In January 1967, the Red Guards organised mass meetings of millions of working people. The mass meetings were part of a 'January Revolution' which swept away the revisionist rule of the CCP and replaced it with a democratic commune representing the workers of Shanghai.

Mao was concerned about the creation of the commune. Its slogan was 'Do away with all heads', which meant that the Red Guards wanted to abolish all leaders. Mao condemned the slogan, as he wanted to regain control. He encouraged the Shanghai Red Guards to work with the PLA and the CCP to restore order to the city.

Source B

A photograph of *The January Storm*, a revolutionary ballet performed in Shanghai in 1967. The ballet was staged by Red Guards to celebrate the creation of the Shanghai Commune.

Revolutionary committees

During 1967, committees made up of Red Guards, PLA officers and surviving members of the CCP took control of major cities. The creation of new revolutionary committees was a first step towards restoring Mao's control. Moreover, it was significant because it indicated that the purge of the CCP was over. Mao ordered that slogans about rebellion should be replaced by slogans stressing loyalty to the PLA.

The PLA takes control

The PLA quickly established control of the revolutionary committees. Mao believed that the PLA was loyal to him, and therefore trusted it to re-establish government. While the PLA played the dominant role in the new revolutionary committees, rival factions of the Red Guards continued to fight on the streets.

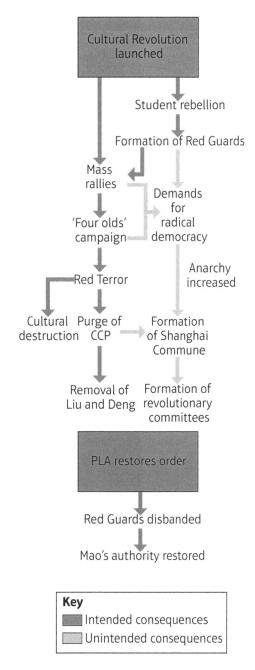

Figure 3.4 The consequences of the Cultural Revolution, 1966–69.

Interpretation 1

From *The Cambridge History of China* by Denis Twitchett and John K. Fairbank, published in 1991.

His [Mao's] personal authority gave him enough power to unleash potent social forces, but not enough power to control them. And his confidence that the masses … would be the salvation of the country proved woefully misplaced as the mass movement degenerated into violence, factionalism, and chaos. The Cultural Revolution … became the monumental error of his latter years.

Interpretation 2

From *China Under Mao, a Revolution Derailed*, by Andrew G. Walder, published in 2015.

The popular insurgency, however, was not left to its own devices. One of the primary functions of the CCRG [Cultural Revolution Group] was to monitor activities on campuses, instigate and support rebellion, and actively undermine serving officials through back-channel communication and encouragement. The CCRG attempted to run the mass movement …

Mao and the CCRG utilised this intelligence network to monitor trends in the student movement, [and] steer it in desired directions …

Exam-style question, Section B

How far do you agree with Interpretation 1 about the extent to which Mao was in control of the Red Terror in the period 1966–68?

Explain your answer using Interpretations 1 and 2 and your knowledge of the historical context.

16 marks

Exam tip

When answering this kind of question, be sure to support your judgement with evidence and argument.

The rise and fall of Lin Biao

At the beginning of the Cultural Revolution, the CCP appointed Lin Biao as Mao's successor. By 1969, Lin was at the height of his power. He made the main speech at the 1969 CCP National Congress and, by mid-1969, his supporters had 49% of the seats on the Central Committee.

Source C

From a press release from the CCP from the Ninth National Party Congress, published on 1 April 1969.

Chairman Mao and his close comrade-in-arms Comrade Lin Biao mounted the rostrum at 5 p.m. sharp. Prolonged thunderous applause resounded throughout the hall. The delegates cheered most enthusiastically 'Long live Chairman Mao!' ... 'Long live the victory of the great proletarian cultural revolution!' and 'Long live the invincible thought of Mao Tse-tung [Zedong]!' ...

Comrade Lin Biao made the political report to the congress. In the report, Comrade Lin Biao, in accordance with Chairman Mao's theory on continuing the revolution under the dictatorship of the proletariat, summed up the basic experience of the great proletarian cultural revolution ...

Activities ?

1 List at least three things you can learn from Source C about Lin Biao's position in the CCP.

2 List two inferences you could make from Source C about Lin's authority in the CCP in 1969.

3 Write a short paragraph to explain how useful Source C is for a historian investigating the consequences of the Cultural Revolution.

Lin's rise was short-lived. Indeed, during the National Party Congress of April 1969, Mao became suspicious that Lin might use the PLA to take power.

One reason for Lin's fall was the influence of Zhou Enlai. During 1969, Mao began to work closely with Zhou. Zhou was an experienced minister who had remained loyal to Mao during the 1960s and therefore escaped being purged during the Cultural Revolution. Zhou argued that the PLA had grown too powerful and that it was time to rebuild the CCP.

Source D

A photograph of Zhou Enlai, Mao Zedong and Lin Biao at a mass meeting in Tiananmen Square in 1967. The photograph was taken by a Chinese press photographer.

The CCP and the PLA

Following the purge of Liu and Deng, Mao decided it was time to revive and rebuild the CCP. In practice, this meant that the PLA became less important, which in turn meant that Lin played a smaller role in government.

Lin attempted to slow down the revival of the CCP, but he failed. Indeed, Mao and Zhou brought many of the people purged during the Cultural Revolution back into the CCP and into the centre of government.

Extend your knowledge

Zhou Enlai

As a university student in the 1920s, Zhou travelled across Europe. He worked with the CCP from the time he returned to China in 1924. Following the Chinese Revolution, Zhou played a key role in government. As Mao's foreign minister he established good relations with countries in Africa and Latin America, such as Tanzania, Peru and Mexico. He was Mao's main ally in rebuilding the CCP after 1969. He was a genuinely popular politician. Indeed, on his death in 1976, crowds of mourners filled Tiananmen Square, leading to protests against radicals in the government.

Activities ?

1 Make a timeline to show the main events of the Cultural Revolution from 1965 to 1971.

2 Explain who or what each of the following were, in a sentence: Zhou Enlai, the Twenty-Three Articles, Wu Nan, revolutionary committees, the Five Man Group, the Shanghai Commune and Project 571.

3 Choose three people from your class to talk – without hesitation, repetition or deviation – about the Red Guards, the purge of the CCP, and the rise and fall of Lin Biao. The person who can talk for the longest wins. Afterwards, list the key facts about each one.

Lin's death

Lin's authority decreased as Mao and Zhou Enlai revived the CCP. However, Lin was still acknowledged as Mao's successor, and therefore was still held in high regard by the Chinese people.

This all changed at the end of 1971, when the Chinese media announced that Lin had been involved in a plot to assassinate Mao. According to the media, after Lin's plot, known as Project 571, was discovered, he had been killed in a aeroplane crash while trying to escape to the USSR. The full details of Lin's death are still secret, so it is impossible to be sure that the Chinese government's account is true.

The social effects of the Cultural Revolution

The Cultural Revolution had profound social effects on China. First, it led to widespread killings and misery:

- The CCP officially estimated that around 36,000 people died as a result of the Cultural Revolution. Independent experts put the figure at about 400,000 deaths.
- Millions were tortured, imprisoned or forced into internal exile.

The Cultural Revolution predominantly affected China's cities. Indeed, throughout the Revolution, Mao discouraged any revolutionary activity that had the potential to disrupt agricultural production.

Some of Mao's ideological goals were met during the Cultural Revolution. For example, rural healthcare, which had been cut back under Liu and Deng, was expanded (see page 130).

Fleeing a purge
Some historians argue that Lin was not involved in a plot against Mao. Rather, they suggest that Lin was fleeing China before Mao could purge him from government.

Destination
Other historians question Lin's destination. Some claim that Lin was intending to flee to Taiwan rather than the USSR.

Working with the USSR
Some Chinese officials claimed that Lin was working with the Soviet secret police to assassinate Mao.

Figure 3.5 Theories about Lin Biao's death.

The impact on education

In the short term, the Cultural Revolution disrupted China's schools and universities massively.

- Universities closed in 1966, as students joined the Red Guards and took part in Mao's revolution.
- Academics were persecuted. Many were killed, tortured or forced to work on farms, such as the May 7th Cadre schools, in order to renew their revolutionary spirit.
- Schools were also affected as younger students joined the Red Guards and attacked their teachers.

Most universities were to remain closed until 1972.

Exam-style question, Section B

How useful are Sources F and G for an enquiry into the impact of the Cultural Revolution on education? Explain your answer, using Sources F and G and your knowledge of the historical context. **8 marks**

Exam tip

When considering how useful sources are, be sure to focus on the subject of the enquiry. Consider the information the sources provide and think about how the purpose of the source might affect its usefulness. Don't forget to consider the historical context.

Source E

A photograph of a PLA soldier educating students in the countryside. The photograph was published by the official Chinese press agency in 1971.

Source F

From an interview with a male student who had been at Amoy University in 1966. He was interviewed in 1971 by a Canadian researcher. The student was in his final year of studying chemistry and was an active member of the Communist Youth League. Amoy University is in Fujian province, which is over 3,000 kilometres from Beijing.

When the first big character poster appeared in Peking [Beijing], we didn't really know what to do. Peking seemed a long way off, and so we waited cautiously for the provincial Party leadership to respond. Who could have predicted that a few months later we would be toppling these leaders and dragging the powerful Ye Fei and his wife out to face mass public criticism ...

All classes were stopped, and the university was in confusion. ... What were we supposed to do? ... The safest course was to attack the most visible targets — the teachers ...

Source G

From an interview with a lecturer at Tsinghua University, in Beijing, published in April 1969. The interview appeared in the *Peking Review*, which was published by the CCP.

One lecturer regarded the re-education he got from the workers' propaganda team as the 'turning point' in his life. Before the great cultural revolution, he had buried himself in vocational work, remained aloof from politics ... Educated and helped by the workers' propaganda team, he arrived at a deep understanding of our great leader Chairman Mao's brilliant teaching ... Angrily denouncing Liu Shao-chi [Liu Shaoqi] and his agents who had poisoned him, he said: 'If we do not arm our minds with Chairman Mao's theories ... we have no soul and will lose our bearings!'

Long-term impact

Mao attempted to address educational problems in a series of reforms during and after the Cultural Revolution:

- Educational funding for well-off students in the cities was reduced, and educational funding for poor students in rural areas was increased.
- The government introduced five years of compulsory education across the whole of China, which benefited

rural areas where access to education had been limited. As a result, there was a 15-fold increase in rural primary schools from 1965 to 1976.

- Educational opportunities for poor peasants and urban workers were expanded. This was achieved by changing the admissions procedures for universities. From 1972 to 1976, universities considered references rather than test scores. This helped students from poorer schools, who tended to perform less well in standard tests.

These reforms led to a better educated population:

- Adult literacy rose from 43% in 1964 to 65% in 1982.
- The literacy of young people also improved. By 1981, 91% of people aged between 15 and 19 were literate, compared to just 56% of people of this age in India, a similar developing country.

Economic effects of the Cultural Revolution

The Cultural Revolution disrupted industry significantly. Indeed, as the Cultural Revolution was a largely urban campaign, it tended to affect industry much more than agriculture.

The most obvious impact of the chaos was a major decline in industrial output. In 1967, industrial production dropped by 13%. While production increased, and was back to its 1965 level by 1971, in the short term there was high urban unemployment, meaning there were few jobs for young people leaving school and university.

Changes in industry

Mao claimed that the Cultural Revolution was designed to empower workers by ending the power and privileges of experts and managers.

The removal of technicians

Technicians, experts and managers had been some of the first victims of the Cultural Revolution. Millions were beaten, killed, imprisoned or exiled to labour camps or farms in Xinjiang province or northern Manchuria. Technicians were attacked because they tended to receive higher pay than workers. As a result, Maoist

Source H

A propaganda poster entitled 'Scatter the old world, build a new world'. The poster was produced by the Cultural Revolution Group in 1967.

propaganda had described technicians, experts and managers as 'bourgeois'.

Impact on workers

In the longer term, surviving technicians and managers were allowed to return to their factories. Nonetheless, there were attempts to make factories more egalitarian. These included:

- the abolition of bonuses and overtime payments
- the reduction of the number of people involved in factory administration
- workers were allowed to play a role in the management of the factories in which they worked
- experts and managers were required to spend at least one-third of their time involved directly in production.

These reforms were introduced in 1969, and temporarily led to a more egalitarian working environment. However, the reforms were phased out by 1972 in order to promote economic growth.

The result was that inequalities between workers and technical experts were as evident after the Cultural Revolution as they had been under Liu and Deng. For example, at one factory in Beijing in 1972, managers were paid three times as much as workers. Nonetheless, Chinese industry was much more egalitarian than other developing countries in Asia, such as Malaysia or developed countries.

Impact on farming

The Cultural Revolution was designed, in part, to put an end to Liu and Deng's 'capitalist road'. In practice, this meant that private farming was reduced.

- By 1966, around 15% of farmland was farmed privately. As a result of the Cultural Revolution, about two-thirds of privately farmed land was returned to the communes. An official limit was introduced that kept private farming to 5% of agricultural land.
- Additionally, privately farmed goods could no longer be traded freely. Rather, the government set the prices of all farm produce.

The move to the countryside

- Finally, the Cultural Revolution led to the establishment of more small industry in rural areas. Mao encouraged the growth of small workshops that fixed tools and farm machinery, as well as small factories that produced fertiliser or cement.

The initiative was broadly successful. Indeed, by 1976, around half of the fertiliser used on farms was being produced locally. What is more, by 1976, around 20 million peasants were involved in local industrial production.

Overall, the Cultural Revolution led to some economic improvements in rural areas. The rural economy grew at around 3% per year during the Cultural Revolution.

Activity ?

Create a diagram showing the main impacts of the Cultural Revolution.

Summary

- By mid-1967, the Cultural Revolution had achieved Mao's primary political aim of eliminating Liu and Deng from the government.
- Reforms in 1969 attempted to make farming, education and industry more egalitarian.
- Reforms in education were broadly successful. Early industrial reforms were less successful and phased out.
- Lin Biao died in mysterious circumstances and was denounced as a traitor.

Checkpoint

Strengthen

S1 Describe two ways in which the Cultural Revolution created problems for Mao in 1967.

S2 Describe two successful reforms introduced as a result of the Cultural Revolution.

S3 Outline the different stages of the development of the Cultural Revolution from 1966 to 1971.

Challenge

C1 Explain how far the Cultural Revolution achieved Mao's political and ideological aims.

C2 In your own words, summarise the significance of the Cultural Revolution in the years 1966–71.

If you are not confident about any of these questions, look over your notes from this section. Your teacher can also give you some hints.

3.4 Winding down the Cultural Revolution, 1968–76

Learning outcomes

- Understand how the Red Guards ended.
- Understand how the authority of the CCP was restored.
- Understand the rise and fall of the Gang of Four.

Timeline

The Cultural Revolution winds down

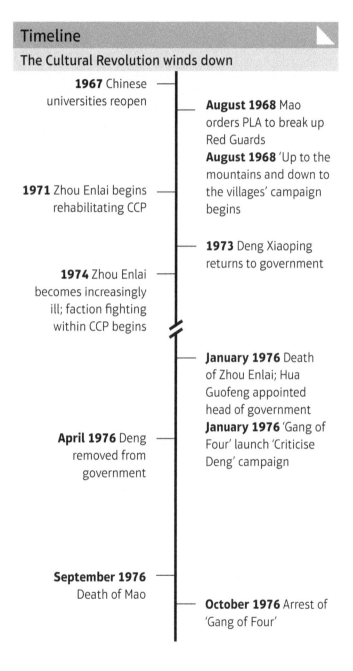

1967 Chinese universities reopen

August 1968 Mao orders PLA to break up Red Guards

August 1968 'Up to the mountains and down to the villages' campaign begins

1971 Zhou Enlai begins rehabilitating CCP

1973 Deng Xiaoping returns to government

1974 Zhou Enlai becomes increasingly ill; faction fighting within CCP begins

January 1976 Death of Zhou Enlai; Hua Guofeng appointed head of government

January 1976 'Gang of Four' launch 'Criticise Deng' campaign

April 1976 Deng removed from government

September 1976 Death of Mao

October 1976 Arrest of 'Gang of Four'

The end of the Red Guards

The Red Guards had played the key role in purging Mao's enemies by persecuting Liu and Deng's supporters. Nonetheless, Mao had never had full control over the Red Guards. By early 1967, it was clear that the Red Guards were becoming more radical than Mao had intended. Radical Red Guards were fighting for a more democratic form of communism, whereas Mao intended to revive the dictatorship of the CCP.

Mao needed to find a way of dissolving the Red Guards in order to restore order and rebuild the CCP under his undisputed leadership. Mao tried a series of strategies. By late 1968, the Red Guards had ceased to be an important force in Chinese politics, and the power of the CCP had been largely restored.

Early attempts to demobilise the Red Guards

Mao's first attempt to disband the Red Guards came in late 1967, when universities were officially reopened. Mao hoped that Red Guards would voluntarily return to their studies and that the movement would disperse. However, this strategy failed, as young people preferred to continue their revolutionary activities.

Mao ordered the demobilisation* of the Red Guards in the spring of 1968. However, many young radicals wanted to continue their political work, and the majority of the Red Guards remained active.

Key term

Demobilise*

Withdraw from combat or military activities and, sometimes, return to civilian life.

The restoration of order by the PLA

By mid-1968, Mao was determined to break up the Red Guards by force. Violence at Beijing University prompted Mao to issue a statement condemning the Red Guards. Mao argued that the Red Guards had lost sight of the goals of the Cultural Revolution and therefore needed to be suppressed. During August 1968, Mao sent propaganda teams backed by elite PLA squads into universities and colleges to break up the Red Guards. Mao justified the change in policy by arguing that the Cultural Revolution was entering a new phase that should be led by the PLA and workers.

Interpretation 1

From *Party vs. State in Post-1949 China* by Shiping Zheng, published in 1997.

A military takeover was neither what Mao's Cultural Revolution was about, nor what Mao had believed to be the appropriate way for reorganising China. Although Mao had no choice but to bring in the military to restore order, he had no intention of letting the military run the country for long. …

Lin Biao's death in 1971 removed a major obstacle to restoring the Party control. The Party had come back, 're-educated' perhaps, but not much different from what it had been before as far as the Party organisation was concerned.

The 'Up to the mountains and down to the villages' campaign

The final demobilisation of the Red Guards took place due to the 'Up to the mountains and down to the villages' campaign. Mao argued that the violence of the Red Guards showed that students needed discipline. He ordered the PLA to transport millions of students to the countryside. Mao justified this by arguing that the students would learn true revolutionary discipline from the peasants. Around 17 million young people were exiled to the countryside in this way between 1968 and 1976. There was some resistance, but it was easily suppressed by the PLA. Many young people never returned to the cities or completed their studies.

Source A

A photograph of former university students working on a farm in Jilin province in 1968. The photograph was published by the CCP.

The 'Up to the mountains and down to the villages' campaign protected the CCP from the threat of continued student revolt. The campaign also dealt with the problem of urban unemployment that had grown in 1968, particularly among young people, due to the disruption caused by the Red Terror.

Source B

From the memoir of Lu Xin, a female novelist, published in 2013. Lu was a student at the beginning of the Cultural Revolution and quickly joined the Red Guards. She volunteered to take part in the 'Up to the mountains and down to the villages' campaign.

I was taught the most honourable way of living was to be a member of the working class ... Some now claim that the Up to the Mountains and Down to the Villages movement was Mao's attempt to get dangerous elements out of the cities. But Mao's policy was consistent with his attitude towards knowledge and education. He always believed intellectuals should serve workers and peasants.

Source C

From Yihong Pan's memoir, published in 2003. Yihong grew up in Beijing. At the age of 16 he was sent to be re-educated on a PLA-run farm in 1969 as part of the 'Up to the mountains and down to the villages' campaign.

Little did I expect that a disciplined life would be so tough. Re-education under the People's Liberation Army meant strict control in every aspect of our lives. All army farms laid down a series of rules: ... no reading ... books ... banned during the Cultural Revolution, ... no singing of ... foreign songs, folk songs or traditional music, ... no courtship within the first three years after one's arrival. ... From morning till night, every detail of life was regulated; even going to the washroom seemed to be scheduled ...

Exam-style question, Section B

How useful are Sources B and C for an enquiry into the experience of young people who were involved in the 'Up to the mountains and down to the villages' campaign?

Explain your answer, using Sources B and C and your knowledge of the historical context. **8 marks**

Exam tip

When considering how useful sources are, consider the information the sources provide and how the nature or purpose of the source weakens or strengthens the evidence.

Activities ?

1 Create a storyboard of the events of the Cultural Revolution, but leave three spaces blank at the start.

2 Look back at pages 77 and 78 about the causes of the Cultural Revolution. Use this information to fill in the three blank spaces at the start of the storyboard.

3 In Interpretation 1, Shiping Zheng argues that, by 1971, the CCP was back in charge of China. Make a list the changes, and the aspects of Chinese government that stayed the same, as a result of the Cultural Revolution.

The increased influence of Zhou Enlai

Having dealt with the Red Guards, Mao was able to revive the power of the CCP. Since Liu and Deng had been removed from the leadership, Mao once again had faith that the CCP was on the road to socialism. He now wanted to restore a properly functioning government.

Zhou Enlai and the CCP

Zhou Enlai was Mao's main ally in reviving the CCP until 1973. Zhou was a talented administrator and Mao trusted him to re-establish the CCP's authority. While there were attempts to reform agriculture and industry, there were few reforms in the structure of the CCP. Under Zhou's leadership:

- CCP officials continued to receive higher pay than workers and peasants
- senior CCP officials continued to enjoy privileges such as free meals, expenses, chauffeur-driven cars, long holidays and access to luxury goods.

Following the death of Lin Biao in 1971, Zhou began to reinstate CCP officials who had been purged during the Cultural Revolution, many of whom were still in prison or who had been sent to work on farms. Zhou began this by publicly criticising Lin Biao. He claimed that Lin Biao and the PLA had persecuted many loyal members of the CCP, and that it was now time that they returned to the government.

THINKING HISTORICALLY — Interpretations (2c/3a)

History as hypotheses

In science, you might have come across the idea of a hypothesis – a hypothesis is an idea that a scientist comes up with to explain what they can see happening. The scientist then tries to find evidence, through experiments, to find out whether their hypothesis is correct. Historians often work in a similar way, but look at sources to find their evidence, rather than doing experiments.

These three historians are thinking about the reasons for the launch of the 'Up to the mountains and down to the villages' campaign.

Historian's interests	Historian's hypothesis	Evidence
Political historian: Interested in leaders, their views and actions and the effects these had on history.	Mao wanted to re-establish the power of the CCP by removing the rebellious Red Guards.	
Economic historian: Interested in how economic conditions changed, and how this affected politics and society.		
Historian of ideas: Interested in ideology and how it affects politics and society.		

Work in groups of three.

1   Make a copy of the above table.

   a   As a group, discuss the interests of each of the historians, and write a hypothesis that they might put forward, based on their interests. (The political historian's hypothesis has been done for you as an example.)

   b   Each person in the group should take on the role of one of the historians. For your historian, add at least three pieces of evidence into the table that support your hypothesis, based on the information and sources in this chapter.

   c   For your historian, write a concluding paragraph, summing up your views on the reasons for the launch of the 'Up to the mountains and down to the villages' campaign. Remember to restate your hypothesis and support it with your evidence.

2   Share your concluding paragraphs with the rest of the group and compare them.

   a   Underline instances where different hypotheses use the same or similar evidence.

   b   Look at each hypothesis in turn. Can you think of at least one piece of evidence that challenges each hypothesis? (Tip: you can start by looking at evidence for the other hypotheses being right!)

3   Discuss as a group: Is it possible to say which hypothesis is correct?

Source D

A photograph of Zhou Enlai, with Jiang Qing (left), meeting Red Guards at a mass rally in Tiananmen Square in 1966.

In 1972 and 1973, Zhou ensured that almost 700 senior members of the CCP who had been purged returned to their jobs. Additionally, he brought back over 150 senior military officers who had been purged by Lin.

Zhou's policy of allowing CCP officials to return to their posts meant that the CCP regained many experienced administrators. This helped restore the efficiency of the CCP, an important step in strengthening the government after the Cultural Revolution. By the end of 1973, the vast majority of government departments were being led by the CCP officials who had led them in 1965.

The return to power of Deng Xiaoping

Deng Xiaoping was the most senior CCP official that Zhou was able to rehabilitate*. In March 1973, Zhou persuaded Mao to overturn Deng's conviction for being China's second most treacherous 'capitalist roader' (after Liu). By August, Deng was reinstated as a member of the Central Committee, a member of the Politburo, and vice

Key term

Rehabilitate*

To restore to a former life or privileges. In terms of Chinese politics, rehabilitation refers to the process by which politicians who had been purged from the CCP were allowed to return to the Party. The word implies that someone has been restored, or purified.

premier. Consequently, Deng was, once again, one of the most powerful figures in the CCP.

Deng was soon playing an important role at the top of government. In January 1975, he was appointed head of the PLA and vice-chairman of the Party Central Committee.

The significance of Deng's return

Deng's return was significant because it indicated that the radicalism of the Cultural Revolution was over. Moreover, it indicated that Mao was, once again, adopting a more pragmatic approach to government.

Deng's return to government was also important because, by 1974, Zhou was old, ill and not expected to recover. Mao, too, was unwell and unable to participate in the day-to-day running of government. Therefore, by the end of 1975, Deng was effectively leading the government.

Interpretation 2

From *Burying Mao: Chinese Politics in the Age of Deng Xiaoping*, by Richard Baum, published in 1996.

After spending seven years in Cultural Revolution ignominy [disgrace], Deng Xiaoping was rehabilitated and restored to favour at the Tenth Party Congress in 1973. On the joint recommendation of Ye Jianying and Zhou Enlai, and with the explicit approval of Chairman Mao, Deng was elevated to the posts of vice-chairman of the party's Military Affairs Commission and vice-premier of the State Council. In January 1975 he was also named PLA chief of staff and vice-chairman of the party Central Committee.

Deng's restoration was deemed necessary to help bolster China's fragile political-military stability.

The rise and fall of the 'Gang of Four'

Zhou and Deng's attempt to strengthen the CCP was not supported by radicals in the government. The leading radicals were headed by a group which became known as the 'Gang of Four' (see Figure 3.6). All four were members of the Politburo, and therefore played a key role in the CCP.

Jiang Qing

An intellectual who was interested in Chinese culture.

She had played a key role in encouraging radicalism during the Cultural Revolution.

Jiang was also Mao's wife.

Zhang Chunqiao

A writer and member of the Cultural Revolution Group.

Zhang was a key ally of Jiang's during the Cultural Revolution.

He had been the leader of the Shanghai Commune.

Yao Wenyuan

Originally a literary critic.

His criticism of the play *Hai Jui dismissed from office* was a trigger for the Cultural Revolution.

He worked on propaganda for the Politburo.

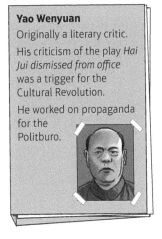

Wang Hongwen

Had been a member of the Red Guards.

Was involved in creating the Shanghai Commune.

By 1976, he was vice-chairman of the CCP.

Figure 3.6 The 'Gang of Four'.

Faction fighting

Zhou's rapidly declining health triggered a power struggle in the party. The 'Gang of Four' wanted the CCP to launch a new Cultural Revolution, whereas Deng wanted to continue Zhou's pragmatic policies. At first, Mao was supportive of Deng, and it seemed he would be Zhou's successor.

The 'Gang of Four' tried various strategies to discredit Deng, including a campaign to encourage people to read the writings of Karl Marx. There was a limited wave of terror in which Deng's supporters at lower levels of the Party were arrested or publicly humiliated.

Following Zhou's death in January 1976, the Gang had a major victory. Mao now supported the Gang's 'Criticise Deng' campaign, which accused Deng of being a 'capitalist roader' and a revisionist. The Gang achieved a second victory in April 1976, when Mao agreed to sack Deng from all of his high-level jobs.

Interpretation 3

From *The Politics of China: The Eras of Mao and Deng* by Roderick MacFarquhar, published in 1997.

When in October [1975] Mao revealed his intention of putting Deng in charge of the country, the Gang of Four were spurred into furious activity to try to deflect the Chairman from his purpose. … the Gang alleged that Zhou was shamming illness and secretly plotting in the hospital with Deng … Mao rejected their protests, praising Deng's ability. … and proposed to implement his earlier suggestion that Deng be made … PLA chief of staff.

Source E

A propaganda poster entitled 'The Great Proletarian Cultural Revolution must be waged to the end'. It was published in 1973 by the CCP.

要把无产阶级文化大革命进行到底

The death of Mao

Mao had become increasingly ill from 1974. For much of 1976 he was unable to speak, forcing him to withdraw from government. Mao's ill health led to the intense faction fighting between the pragmatists and the 'Gang of Four'. In January 1976, Mao appointed Hua Guofeng as head of government. Hua was part of neither faction, and his appointment gave neither side the advantage. Mao died in September 1976, with the struggle to control the government unresolved.

The arrest of the 'Gang of Four'

Immediately following Mao's death, the 'Gang of Four' began a propaganda campaign claiming that they were Mao's rightful heirs. At the same time, the Gang gave orders to its supporters in Shanghai to arm the militia. Some historians have argued that this indicates that the Gang was preparing to seize power by force.

Fearing that the Gang was about to launch a coup, Hua, the Politburo and the leaders of the PLA agreed to arrest the Gang and its main supporters. Less than a month after Mao's death, the 'Gang of Four' was removed from the government and its hopes of seizing power were thwarted. Hua and his supporters succeeded in destroying the 'Gang of Four', but failed to hold on to power. Deng Xiaoping re-emerged as a powerful figure in the CCP in 1977, and by the end of 1978 was effectively leader of China.

Activities ?

1 Draw a spider diagram to show the key features of the power struggle in the years before Mao's death. Describe each feature in 10 words or less.

2 Write a sentence explaining the visions of the rival groups.

3 Put yourself in the shoes of a citizen of Beijing who lived through the 1950s and 1960s. Write a list of what you want from the future. Write a paragraph explaining which possible leader of China is most likely to give you what you want.

Summary

- During 1967 and 1968, Mao used a variety of techniques to demobilise the Red Guards.
- From 1969, Mao relied on Zhou Enlai to rebuild the power of the CCP.
- Zhou reinstated many of the CCP officials who had been purged during the Cultural Revolution.
- Faction fighting intensified in the CCP during 1976 as Mao's health deteriorated.
- The 'Gang of Four' failed in its attempt to seize control of the CCP.
- In the years after Mao's death in 1976, Deng Xiaoping was restored to power.

Checkpoint

Strengthen

S1 Outline the different stages by which Mao demobilised the Red Guards in the years 1967–68.

S2 Describe two ways in which Zhou revived the CCP.

S3 Outline the different stages of the development of the Cultural Revolution from 1965 to 1976.

Challenge

C1 Explain why you think Mao wanted to strengthen the CCP in the years 1969–76.

C2 Explain why you think the 'Gang of Four' wanted to remove Deng in 1976.

If you can't answer any of the questions, visit your school learning resource centre to find more information.

Recap: The Cultural Revolution and its aftermath, 1966–76

Recall quiz

1 Where were the mass rallies held in 1966?

2 List three reasons why Mao launched the Cultural Revolution.

3 Define 'capitalist road'.

4 Which two senior leaders did Mao want to remove in the Cultural Revolution?

5 What did Mao mean by his order to 'bombard the headquarters'?

6 Why was the Five Man Group formed?

7 When did Liu Shaoqi die?

8 How did Lin Biao die?

9 When did Deng Xiaoping re-enter the government?

10 Who did Mao appoint as head of government in January 1976?

Activity ?

Copy and complete the following table outlining the views of the 'Gang of Four' and the pragmatists.

The 'Gang of Four'	The pragmatists, such as Liu, Zhou and Deng

Activities ?

1 Using the information in this section, hold a debate on the statement: 'The Cultural Revolution failed to achieve Mao's ideological aims.'

2 Design two posters:

  a The first should support the 'Gang of Four' and criticise Deng and Zhou's policies.

  b The second should support the arrest of the 'Gang of Four', explaining the problems with their policies.

3 Draw a living graph of Deng Xiaoping's life between 1949 and 1976. List the key events, and show how his power increased and decreased throughout his career.

4 Draw a living graph of Mao's main policies from 1949 to 1976. List the key events and show how pragmatic or idealistic the policies were throughout his rule.

5 Imagine you are a Western journalist writing Mao's obituary in 1976. In no more than 150 words, sum up his main successes, failures and the significance of his rule.

6 Imagine you are a CCP journalist writing Mao's obituary in 1976. In no more than 150 words, sum up his main successes and the significance of his rule.

Writing historically: explaining and evaluating

You need to think about the purpose of your writing to help you structure it and choose how you express your ideas.

Learning outcomes

By the end of this lesson, you will understand how to:
- use the key features of explanatory and analytical writing
- structure your writing to ensure you explain or evaluate effectively.

Definitions

Explain: to make an idea clear using relevant facts, details and examples.

Evaluate: to examine two or more points of view closely and carefully in order to make a judgement or come to a conclusion.

What are the similarities and differences in writing to **explain** and writing to **evaluate**?

Compare these two exam-style questions (note that Question B has been adapted to make reference to Interpretation 2):

Question A

> Explain why Mao launched the Cultural Revolution in 1966. **(12 marks)**

Question B

> How far do you agree with Interpretation 1 (see Interpretation 1 from 3.3.) about the extent to which Mao was in control of the Red Terror in the period 1966–68?
>
> Explain your answer using Interpretations 1 and 2 (see Interpretations 1 and 2 from 3.3.) and your knowledge of the historical context. **(16 marks)**

1. Look at the statements below. Which of them apply to Question A, which to Question B and which to both?
   This kind of question:

   a. asks you to write to explain.

   b. asks you to evaluate.

   c. asks you to consider arguments for and against a point of view and reach a conclusion.

   d. requires you to explain how and why an event happened or a situation came about.

   e. requires you to provide evidence and examples to support your ideas.

   f. requires you to link all your ideas to key points.

   g. requires you to explain at least one sequence of events and their consequences.

   h. requires you to consider what contributed to a situation or event.

   i. requires you to link and develop your ideas logically to form a line of reasoning.

   j. requires you to demonstrate good knowledge and understanding of the features or characteristics of the historical period.

   k. requires you to explore how and why a series of circumstances, events or actions led to a particular outcome.

2. Look at your answers to Question 1. What are the key differences between questions that ask you to 'explain' and questions that ask 'how far do you agree'?

How can I structure writing to explain and writing to evaluate?

3. Answers to 'explain why' questions often follow this structure: 1st point; 2nd point; 3rd point; summary of causes and effects that led to a specific outcome.

The start of some sentences have been written out below in answer to Question A. Put the sentences in the order in which you think they should appear.

> a. Mao's ideas were important because …
>
> b. Mao's ideology was another reason that he launched the Cultural Revolution …
>
> c. Mao launched the Cultural Revolution in 1966, after several years when he had not been in control …
>
> d. Mao's desire to re-establish control of the CCP was also significant …
>
> e. One reason that Mao launched the Cultural Revolution was that he believed that capitalist values needed to be purged from the CCP …

Now look at the plan below for an answer to an exam-style question that asks you to evaluate. Remember, in the exam you need to refer to both interpretations in the question.

1st point to support the interpretation	a. The Red Guards continued to attack the CCP even after Liu and Deng had been purged …
2nd point to support the interpretation	b. The Shanghai Commune, established in January 1967 …
Signal a turning point in the argument	c. However, Interpretation 2 argues …
1st point to contradict the interpretation	d. Mao's supporters on the Cultural Revolution Group kept control of the Red Guards …
2nd point to contradict the interpretation	e. Mao used the Red Guards to eliminate his enemies …
Conclusion: a judgement directly responding to the interpretation	f. So, there are different ways to assess the extent of Mao's control of the Red Guards. Interpretation 1 is correct in the sense that …

4. Look at these exam-style questions:

> Explain why Mao launched the 'Up to the mountains and down to the villages' campaign. **(12 marks)**
>
> How far do you agree with Interpretation 1 (see Interpretation 1 in 2.2) about the causes of the Great Famine of 1958–62?
>
> Explain your answer using both Interpretations 1 and 2 (see Interpretations 1 and 2 in 2.2) and your knowledge of the historical context. **(16 marks)**

Plan an answer to each one, using the same structures as the responses above. Write the first sentence of each paragraph.

04 | Life in Mao's China, 1949–76

The CCP wanted to transform China. The goal was to create a classless society, in which all kinds of inequality were abolished. The CCP claimed that its goal of total transformation meant that it needed total power. It wanted power to create a new kind of family in which all people were equal. It wanted power to create a new and equal relationship between the sexes, in which men and women were free to work and live as they chose. Chinese communists also wanted to establish new forms of art and culture which rejected capitalist values and reflected communist values of equality and selfless devotion to the CCP. Finally, communists wanted to reform the way that Chinese people thought about the world. Indeed, the CCP used a variety of techniques to challenge old-fashioned ideas, related to capitalism, religion and traditional Chinese philosophy, which it believed stood in the way of progress.

The CCP's goal of total transformation justified total power. In practice, this meant CCP control of the media through censorship and propaganda. It also meant the creation of a system of labour camps, designed to re-educate people who refused to embrace Mao's vision of socialism. It also required reforms to education and healthcare, to ensure that all workers had access to the benefits of modern society. Finally, it required control over culture, because Mao believed that culture played a key role in reflecting the values of a new society.

Some of the CCP's attempts to create a better society were successful. Others ended in terrible failures. But there can be no doubt that, by 1976, many aspects of life in China had been transformed.

Learning outcomes

In this chapter, you will find out:

- how use of propaganda, censorship and the labour system were used to create communist control
- how communist rule changed family life and the role of women
- why communist rule changed education and healthcare
- why, and in what ways, communists created a new revolutionary culture.

4.1 Communist control

The CCP used the media to help control China. This included publishing propaganda which supported the government, and censorship* to stop the Chinese people being influenced by alternative points of view.

The CCP controlled the media by ensuring that the CCP or the PLA ran all aspects of the press, radio and film-making. From 1949, large parts of the media were integrated into the CCP and PLA.

Propaganda, censorship and thought control were central to CCP rule. CCP leaders believed it was their mission to liberate the Chinese people. However, they were also worried that workers and peasants were so poorly educated that they could not understand the truth of communism, and might be deceived by capitalists. Therefore, the CCP used a variety of methods to ensure that the people understood communist values.

- **Censorship** prevented the distribution of dangerous ideas that could influence poorly educated people.
- **Propaganda** was designed to present a simplified message and to inspire uneducated workers and peasants to support the CCP and its reforms.
- **Thought control** ensured that influential groups embraced communist ideology.

Key term

Censorship*

The process through which 'undesirable' and dangerous information and ideas are removed from books, newspapers, films or any other media.

Censorship

The CCP used censorship throughout most of Mao's time as leader, and applied it to books, film, music and the arts. However, the nature of censorship changed over that time, as shown in Figure 4.1. Essentially, the Ministry of Culture set up a series of organisations called bureaus, which oversaw censorship across the media.

Throughout the Hundred Flowers campaign (1956), censorship was briefly relaxed. The *People's Daily* newspaper grew from six to eight pages to allow more room for articles from intellectuals who were not CCP members. However, once the campaign was stopped, censorship was reintroduced.

Propaganda

In the early years, Mao argued that propaganda had three main tasks:

- to fill the people with revolutionary spirit
- to teach workers and peasants their tasks
- to educate the people so that they understood the CCP's policies.

In reality, the focus of propaganda changed over time.

- In the early years, CCP leaders used propaganda to encourage people to participate in mass campaigns.
- During the first Five-Year Plan (1953–57) and the Great Leap Forward (1958–62), propaganda was used to inspire workers and peasants to support the government's economic goals.
- During the early 1960s, under Liu Shaoqi and Deng Xiaoping, the media stressed the importance of respecting and obeying authority, particularly the authority of managers, teachers and parents.
- Throughout the Cultural Revolution (1966–76), radicals used the media to try to direct the Red Guards.

	1949–54	1954–64	1964–76
Books	In 1950, the CCP set up the Publications Administration Bureau. The Bureau quickly banned 6,766 of the 8,000 books published in China before the revolution. From 1950, the CCP controlled publishing through the People's Publishing House.	During the Hundred Flowers campaign, pamphlets that were critical of the CCP were allowed to be published. However, the reduction of censorship was short-lived. Publishing freedom was seriously restricted from the start of the 'Anti- Rightist' purge.	During the Cultural Revolution, censorship became even stricter. Red Guards took control of the offices of the People's Publishing House and stopped the publication of all books, except the works of Mao. Red Guards also destroyed books that they believed contained old ideas.
Film	From 1950 to 1954, the Film Bureau focused on banning films that had been made before the revolution.	From the late 1950s, the Film Bureau worked to censor films created in the West and in the USSR. This was often done through dubbing and editing, which removed parts of the script that the Bureau believed were counter-revolutionary.	During the Cultural Revolution, Jiang Qing ordered a new wave of censorship, and 400 films made in the decade before 1964 were banned. Censorship was so strong that between 1965 and 1971 the Chinese film industry effectively stopped production.
Art and music	From 1949, the CCP imposed controls on music composition and the production of painting and sculpture. Mao stated that artists should be cultural soldiers, and only art that served communism was allowed.	The 1960 Congress of Artists laid down new guidelines for the production of art and music. This led to a purge of a great deal of art that had been produced prior to 1960.	Jiang Qing supervised the production of model operas in which the music was composed and designed to honour the revolution. Other forms of artistic work stopped.

Figure 4.1 Censorship in China, 1949–76.

The media

The CCP used a variety of media to get its message across. For example:

- **The press:** The CCP controlled the majority of China's newspapers through the CCP's Propaganda Department. The People's Daily was one of the most important national newspapers, and reflected the views of the CCP's leadership. By 1959, China had 28 national newspapers and 1,427 local newspapers.

- **Radio:** The CCP used radio extensively, because it allowed the Party to communicate with people who could not read. National radio was produced by the Central People's Broadcasting station, which was based in Beijing and supervised directly by the Central Committee. Radio speakers were set up in communal canteens, in school halls, in factories or on poles in fields. The number of speakers shot up from 65,398 in mid-1955 to 6 million in 1964, covering 95% of villages.

- **Film:** Mao believed that film was a very powerful medium. From 1954, the Ministry of Culture organised film production at studios in Changchun, Beijing and Shanghai. By 1965, film was extremely popular. Official reports indicate that the average Chinese peasant saw five films a year.

- **Books:** The CCP controlled book publishing through the People's Publishing House, which produced technical manuals to aid industrialisation and collectivisation. It also produced 'egg books'*, which contained exciting stories of communist heroes.

Key term

Egg books*

Short popular novels. They were called egg books because they were as cheap as eggs.

Source A

A photograph of peasants in Chongqing, now a province of southwest China, unpacking radio equipment in the late 1950s. The photograph was originally published in an American magazine.

Source B

From an article in *People's China*, December 1951. *People's China* was a magazine published to promote the CCP outside of China.

They are called 'egg books' ... you'll find them in every peasant household. ... But last year when the peasants looked to buy the latest batch of booklets, they found them cheap as before but how different! ... The old time heroes — but with a difference, appearing now in their true roles as the heroes of the people. And tales of the heroes of today — labour heroes, volunteers battling the American invaders in Korea; modern inventors; stories of adventures in catching Kuomintang [GMD] spies, tales of love and marriage in the new, emancipated society.

Propagandists and agit-prop

The CCP employed thousands of people as propagandists at both national and local levels. They created agit-prop*, propaganda designed to agitate or excite the Chinese people to action. Propagandists not only created campaigns and slogans, designed posters and wrote articles and pamphlets – they were also employed to perform plays and teach educational classes. No form of media was ignored: even songs and postcards were used to spread Mao's and the CCP's political ideas.

Political messages were carried to people in all parts of the country. For example, peasants had to attend political meetings and watch the performances and films put on by agit-prop touring groups, such as Red Drama Groups (see page 133). The groups' plays used simple plots, such as heroic peasants overcoming wicked landlords, to teach the audience to abandon old customs and accept new ideas.

Key term

Agit-prop*

Short for agitation propaganda.

Propaganda campaigns

Propaganda was an essential part of all of the CCP's campaigns, including the 1950 Resist America, Aid Korea campaign, the first Five-Year Plan and the Cultural Revolution.

The Resist America, Aid Korea campaign

The Resist America, Aid Korea campaign was launched in response to US involvement in the Korean War. It encouraged workers and peasants to aid the war against capitalism in Korea. It persuaded over 2 million volunteers to fight in Korea, while others supported the war effort by working hard to produce weapons and clothing. Importantly, the war and the campaign gave Chinese people a sense of national identity and pride in the communist People's Republic of China.

The campaign against Hu Feng

The campaign against Hu Feng is a good example of the way in which the CCP used propaganda. Following the establishment of the PRC, Hu Feng, a supporter of the communists since 1923, became a member of the National People's Congress. However, Hu was critical of the CCP's cultural policies. In 1955, Hu sent a report, known as the 300,000-word letter, to the Central Committee, criticising Mao's ideas on culture and arguing for greater artistic freedom. As a result, the CCP's Central Propaganda Department launched a campaign against him in order to educate the public about the virtues of Mao's thought and weed out undesirable capitalist ideas.

The propaganda campaign against Hu used posters to depict Hu as a GMD agent who pretended to be a communist. CCP propaganda also claimed that Hu was at the centre of a conspiracy to overthrow the CCP. Therefore, propaganda teams encouraged people to search for supporters of Hu, to humiliate them and to force them to admit their crimes in self-criticism sessions. In so doing, CCP propaganda encouraged people to be suspicious of individualism, non-conformity* and anyone who criticised the CCP or Mao's ideas.

At the end of 1955, Hu, along with 23 others, was found guilty of plotting to overthrow the CCP and sent to a labour camp. The trial and sentence were also used as propaganda to warn of the danger of counter-revolution.

Key term

Non-conformity*

Refusing to live in the usual or approved way.

Source C

From an article by Mao Zedong in the *People's Daily*, July 1955. The *People's Daily* was the official newspaper of the CCP.

If there is anything positive the Hu Feng clique [group] can offer, it is that through the present soul-stirring struggle we shall raise our own political consciousness and sensitivity much higher, firmly suppress all counter-revolutionaries and greatly strengthen our revolutionary dictatorship; we shall thus carry the revolution through to the end and achieve the objective of building a great socialist country.

Source D

A propaganda poster of a PLA soldier arresting Hu Feng. The poster was produced by the CCP's Central Propaganda Department in 1955.

The cult of Lei Feng

During the 1960s, CCP propaganda created the cult* of Lei Feng. Lei was a PLA soldier who, following his death in 1962, was presented to the public as a perfect communist who studied closely Mao's writings. Government propaganda presented Lei as a soldier who was always willing to serve others. Feng's most famous acts included collecting worn-out clothes and mending them, changing a bus tyre so that workers could get to their factory, and helping an elderly woman get home in dangerous conditions. Lei's life was celebrated in:

- the film *Lei Feng*, which was released in 1963
- a series of 12 photographs that depicted some of his good deeds

- a diary which described his activities and his love of Mao.

It is now believed that the stories of his good deeds were invented and the photographs of his actions were faked. Nonetheless, the campaign was highly successful, as millions of Chinese people respected Lei and tried to follow his example of helping others and following Mao without question.

Key term

Cult*

A system of belief in, or devotion to, a person or object.

Activities ?

1. Make a quiz for your classmates, featuring five questions about CCP propaganda and censorship. You must write out the questions and answers in full.

2. Create a flow chart explaining why the CCP wanted to control the Chinese media.

3. Write a paragraph explaining what you can infer about the CCP's approach to propaganda from Sources C and D.

The significance of the 'cult of Mao'

CCP rule was based, in part, on the 'cult of Mao'. The CCP used the media to create a cult of personality. That is to say, propaganda created a heroic image of Mao as an all-knowing, benevolent, revolutionary leader whose ideas were the key to a better future. Posters, busts and statues of Mao were common across China, and books of his writing and speeches were widely available. In this sense, Mao was not simply a political leader, he was regarded as something like a living god.

The 'cult of Mao' was evident years before the CCP took power. From 1945, his thoughts were recognised as the ideology of the CCP. Mao's authority grew from 1949 to 1958 due to the apparent success of his policies. Even after the failure of the Great Leap Forward, Mao was still respected as the founder of the CCP.

The 'cult of Mao' within the CCP

The 'cult of Mao' served an important purpose within the CCP. It gave Mao a status that was above any of the other leaders. Therefore, Mao was above criticism and had the final say when disputes broke out in the CCP.

Studying and understanding Mao's writings were essential for any Party member. For example, the preface to the 'Little Red Book', first produced for the PLA and then made widely available in 1966, directed readers to 'Study Chairman Mao's writings, follow his teachings and act according to his instructions'. Arguments were often settled by referring to his thoughts as set out in the book.

Source E

From the recollections of a young woman who was 21 years old at the time of the Cultural Revolution. Her recollections were published in an oral history of the Cultural Revolution in 1996.

The person I worshipped was Mao Zedong.

And not only me. Go ask anyone of my generation who they worshipped when they were in their twenties. I can assure you, you'd get the same answer from everyone – Mao Zedong. ...

Lin Min, one of Mao's daughters, was my classmate in college. Mao's birthday was on the 26th of December, and one year ... nine coeds living in the same dorm got together to discuss sending him a birthday gift ... We chattered on about this past midnight. ... but still we couldn't come up with a gift that appropriately reflected our ardor [love].

Exam-style question, Section A

Give two things you can infer from Source E about the 'cult of Mao'. **4 marks**

Exam tip

You infer something from a source by working out something the source does not actually tell you directly. In this case, you could consider what the decision to send Mao a birthday present tells you about the cult.

Source F

A propaganda poster, 'Respectfully wish Chairman Mao eternal life'. The poster was produced by the CCP in 1968.

The growing 'cult of Mao', 1965–68

The 'cult of Mao' was the basis of the Cultural Revolution. During it, Mao's supporters argued that the CCP could no longer be trusted to lead the revolution. Rather, they claimed that Mao was the only source of revolutionary authority due to his position as a war hero and defender of China, as well as his vision as a revolutionary leader who cared for the people. Therefore, Mao had the authority to order the Red Guards to attack the CCP, in order to save the revolution, and to order the Red Guards to disband when the Cultural Revolution ended.

The 'cult of Mao' grew greatly during the Cultural Revolution. The 'Little Red Book' gained a mystic status – some Red Guards claimed that it had magical powers. However, as the Cultural Revolution was wound down, the cult lessened. Mao recognised that restoring the authority of the CCP meant limiting his own cult, and restoring confidence in the leaders of government.

Activities ?

In small groups:

1 Skim through the chapters of this book, and look at every propaganda picture of Mao. Make notes about each picture.
2 Make a list of the common features of propaganda pictures of Mao.
3 Design your own propaganda poster of Mao, using as many of the common features as you can.

Thought control

Thought control was an ongoing part of the CCP's strategy for controlling China. Mao, and other leading communists, assumed that different classes naturally formed different ideas about the world. For example, the ideas of landlords and the bourgeoisies were anti-communist. Therefore, the CCP was committed to reforming the ideas of whole classes of the population.

The origins of thought control

Thought control had been part of Chinese tradition for many years before the CCP took power. Indeed, some historians argue that new rulers traditionally had imposed their beliefs on others when they took power. Indeed, Chinese intellectuals had been forced to engage in self-criticism for centuries before Mao took power.

Key term
Thought control*
The process through which people were encouraged to replace one set of ideas with another.

Thought control, 1951

The CCP's first major thought control campaign was launched in September 1951. Zhou Enlai initiated the campaign with a speech in which he emphasised the need for China's bourgeois intellectuals to submit to thought control, as the CCP assumed that intellectuals had capitalist ideas because of their class. Mao wanted the bourgeoisies to think like peasants, who he believed were natural supporters of the revolution.

The campaign began in China's major universities, initially affecting 3,000 university teachers. The thought reform occurred in three stages, in which university teachers were required to publicly:

- confess their selfish capitalist views
- criticise themselves
- engage in political study sessions, where they learnt about Marxism.

The campaign spread quickly to schools and colleges across China.

Source G

A photograph showing people marching during the Cultural Revolution. The photograph was taken by a Chinese press photographer.

The 'Reform Through Labour' system

Mao linked thought reform to re-education through labour. He believed that intellectuals would learn to think like peasants through working like peasants. This idea influenced a large number of CCP policies.

- barefoot doctors (see page 130) were expected to spend half of their time farming, so that they would not become a new class with a higher status than the peasants they served
- following the Cultural Revolution, industrial experts were required to spend one-third of their time engaged in working on the factory floor.

Laogai camps

The *Laogai* camps were the most extreme example of the principle of the 'Reform Through Labour' system. The camps were large forced labour camps. In theory, they were designed to re-educate people who did not understand the benefits of communism through labour. In practice, they were huge concentration camps where millions of prisoners were forced to work in appalling conditions. The camps contained two kinds of prisoner. Around 90% of prisoners were considered politically dangerous. The remaining 10% were criminals or people who owed money to the government.

The *Laogai* camps were built in inaccessible parts of China to discourage escape attempts. Between 1953 and 1955, the prison population grew from 2 million to around 10 million due to increased repression. Around 25 million people died in *Laogai* camps between 1949 and 1976.

Mao's camps played an important economic role. Prison labourers were fed a subsistence diet largely comprising grass soup, and were housed in squalid conditions. They were a source of cheap labour, doing vital work. Some camps produced consumer goods while others were involved in building factories, farming, or hazardous work, such as mining.

Activities ?

1 Write a sentence explaining why the CCP used thought control.
2 Write a paragraph explaining the different types of thought control the CCP used.
3 Which do you think would have been the most effective? Why?

Source H

From a speech by Mao on thought reform given in 1965.

We should take laogai work very seriously, and should not think about making a profit. Do not be concerned about making money off of the prisoners. The focus should be on reform ... Thought reform comes first.

Source I

From the recollections of Harry Wu, an inmate at a *Laogai* camp from 1960 to 1979. Wu's recollections were published in *Writers Under Siege*, a collection of essays about repression published in 2007.

My brain cells were gradually deactivating. All varieties of thoughts and perceptions — memories of childhood, nostalgic recollections of my sweetheart, thoughts of missing my parents, the yearning for freedom, the pursuit of dignity, fear of death, bewilderment over hunger — were receding. ...

The number of people who died after collapsing in the outhouse during bouts of diarrhoea dwindled. Now, more people died on the kangs [sleeping platforms] in their cell blocks, departing without a word.

Exam-style question, Section B

How useful are Sources H and I for an enquiry into the purpose of the *Laogai* system? Explain your answer, using Sources H and I and your knowledge of the historical context. **8 marks**

Exam tip

When analysing and evaluating the utility of the sources you do not need to reach a judgement about which of the sources is more useful.

Summary

- Mao's government used control of the media, propaganda and censorship, as well as thought control and labour camps, to control the population.
- The CCP integrated large parts of the media into the Party in order to control the press, radio, film and books.
- The CCP's media policy changed over time, becoming more ideological during the Cultural Revolution.

Checkpoint

Strengthen

S1 Describe the key features of CCP control of the media.

S2 Explain the reasons why Mao believed that propaganda and censorship were necessary.

S3 Explain the reasons why Mao believed that forced labour could help re-educate the CCP's enemies.

Challenge

C1 In your own words, summarise the role of the 'cult of Mao' in Chinese politics, 1949–76.

C2 'CCP rule relied more on terror than control of the media.' How far do you agree with this statement?

If you can't answer these questions, re-read the sections containing the information you need.

Chinese communists were committed to reforming all aspects of the economy and society in order to end exploitation. This included a commitment to reforming family life and the role of women in society.

Changes in the status of women under Mao

In 1949, traditional views and customs still dominated China. For example, under the 'Three Guiding Principles', or *san gang*, citizens and ministers had to obey their ruler, sons had to obey their fathers, and women had to obey their husbands. Within this male-dominated society, a woman's life was expected to reflect the 'three obediences': obedience to her father during childhood, to her husband as an adult, and to her sons if she was widowed.

Woman and marriage

In most of China, even in 1949, marriage underlined a woman's inferior social status. Most women were forced into arranged marriages*. Weddings were arranged by a 'matchmaker', a woman who checked that both partners were legally entitled to marry, of a similar status and had no disabilities – there was a huge stigma* attached to disability, and therefore disability was considered an obstacle to marriage.

Women were often forced into marriage between the age of 12 and 19. Marriage before the age of 12 was illegal in 1949, but some child marriages did occur in rural areas.

In order to arrange a marriage, a bride's family had to provide a dowry*. Wealthy families provided expensive items, such as jewellery; poor families would give household items like bedding and pots and pans. The dowry emphasised the view that women were an economic burden.

Married life for women

Married life traditionally reflected women's inferior social status. Traditionally, husbands had the right to sell their wives when a married woman had committed adultery or tried to run away. In some areas, polygamy – marrying more than one person – was widespread, as were households where a husband would have a wife and one or more concubines*. Married women were expected to do all the unpaid domestic labour, such as cooking, cleaning and childcare.

Female infanticide

Extremely poor families would sometimes resort to female infanticide: killing a female baby soon after birth, in order to avoid having to support it. Families assumed that male babies would grow up to work and contribute to the family, whereas female babies would marry early and require a dowry, making them a financial drain. In 1949, estimates suggest that around 5% to 10% of female babies were killed or died of neglect.

Key terms

Arranged marriage*

A form of marriage in which a bride and groom are selected for each other by their families. The couple are forced to marry by social pressure.

Stigma*

Extreme social disapproval, which tends to lead to people being isolated and poorly treated.

Dowry*

A transfer of property from the bride's family to the husband, that takes place when a couple get married.

Concubines*

Women who live with a man, but are not married to him, and have a lower social status than his wife or wives.

The significance of foot binding

In 1949, foot binding, which had been outlawed since 1912, was still common in rural areas. Foot binding was the custom of preventing women's feet from growing by bandaging them tightly. Binding was incredibly painful and caused distortion of the feet. Foot binding was considered to make women more beautiful.

Activities ?

1 In groups, discuss attitudes to women in China in 1949 and how traditional customs reinforced these attitudes.

2 Decide on one social change that you think would most help to change attitudes to Chinese women.

3 Write a CCP campaign slogan and design a poster to promote this change.

Reasons for change under Mao

Mao had been influenced by the Chinese feminist movement early in his life and was therefore an advocate of equal rights for women. He believed that women's liberation was an essential part of creating a socialist society. Mao believed:

- that men and women both needed to be educated and to work in order to modernise China
- that socialism should end all oppression, including the oppression of women
- that traditional forms of marriage were oppressive. Indeed, Mao had been forced into an arranged marriage as a young man, and therefore had personal experience of the nature of traditional customs.

While Mao was committed to gender equality, his policies never led to full equality between men and women.

The significance of changes

Ending foot binding and reforming marriage law led to significant changes in the status of women.

Ending foot binding

The abolition of foot binding was a clear success. By the end of 1950, foot binding had virtually disappeared across the whole of China. Significantly, the introduction of the communes and the horrors of the great famine, which led to a step backwards for the rights of women, did not lead to a reintroduction of foot binding.

The Marriage Law, 1950

The Marriage Law of 1950 was an important step towards improving women's status, abolishing 'feudal' (traditional) marriage laws. The new law:

- outlawed forced marriages and ended the rights of 'matchmakers'
- outlawed the marriage of children, bigamy*, men living with concubines, and dowries
- introduced equal legal status between husband and wife within families
- introduced equal property rights, so that women could own and inherit property on an equal basis to men
- legalised divorce and ended wife-selling
- outlawed maltreatment of women within households.

The PLA enforced the new laws across China, leading to an improvement in the status of women.

Women's property rights were enforced as part of land reform. The PLA distributed property to men and women. The PLA also punished former landlords for mistreating women. This was intended to send the message that women's rights should be respected.

Key term

Bigamy*
The practice of marrying multiple partners.

Female infanticide

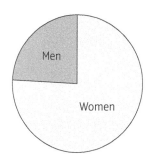

The rate of female infanticide (killing of female babies) dropped from as much as 10% in 1949 to 2% in 1960.

Child marriages

The number of child marriages dropped by 85% between 1949 and 1965.

Divorces

Women initiated 76% of the divorces that were granted during 1951, indicating that the new law was allowing women to become more independent.

Figure 4.2 The impact of CCP policy on women.

Source A

A poster, entitled 'Freedom of marriage, happiness and good luck', published by the CCP in 1953. The book in the background shows the first section of the 1950 Marriage Law.

自由婚姻 美滿幸福

Exam-style question, Section A

Give two things you can infer from Source A about the reasons for the Marriage Law of 1950. **4 marks**

Exam tip

You infer something from a source by working out something the source does not actually tell you directly. In this case, consider the book in the background.

Continuing inequalities and popular attitudes towards women

Women won greater independence as a result of CCP rule. It also led to new opportunities for women to work in towns, because Mao and other CCP leaders viewed female labour as essential to the industrial development of China. However, there were still obstacles to full equality:

- Long-standing prejudice meant that CCP and PLA officials did not always take women's rights seriously.

- In some areas, men refused to accept divorce and imprisoned their former wives.

- Men dominated the CCP. From 1949 to 1965, less than 13% of CCP officials were women.

- During the Cultural Revolution, women were put under huge pressure to be androgynous*. Women who wore traditionally feminine clothes or hairstyles were beaten by Red Guards.
- While levels of female employment increased, women tended to get lower-paid and lower-status jobs. Moreover, men tended to get promoted faster than women, largely due to long-standing prejudices.
- Working women were still expected to do the vast majority of domestic tasks.
- The CCP's policy of investing in heavy industry meant that there were no funds to set up childcare facilities, or laundries that would have cut down women's domestic labour.

Source B

A photograph of women working in a textile factory in Beijing. The photograph was taken by a French photographer travelling in China in 1955.

Activities ?

1 Give CCP policies towards women a mark out of 10 for effectiveness.
2 Discuss your mark – and your reasons – with other people in your class.
3 Write a paragraph justifying your mark.

Key term

Androgynous*

Having an appearance that is neither strongly male, nor strongly female.

Source C

From an article in *People's China*, March 1974. *People's China* was an English-language newspaper published by the CCP to promote communism in other countries.

With the founding of the People's Republic of China ... the Party and Government drew up a constitution ... to guarantee and promote the right of women to enjoy equality with men politically, economically, culturally, socially and in the home. The Marriage Law promulgated in 1950 completely did away with the arbitrary and compulsory feudal marriage system ...

In education, the arts and science and other fields, large numbers of women are working diligently for socialism. All this speaks well for the fact that times have changed and today men and women are equal.

Source D

From the Chinese newspaper *Chinese Women*, published in late 1963. The newspaper was published by the CCP and gave advice to women on how to live their lives.

Housework has to be divided up among the family and each person has to do some of it. It must not be overly concentrated on the female comrade. In this respect if the male comrade's thinking and views are not very correct and still include feudal or bourgeois remnants [old ways of thinking], the female comrade should not be overly accommodating and there is no harm in her carrying out a suitable degree of struggle.

Changes in family life

The CCP aimed to reform the family radically. Communists believed that traditional families encouraged bourgeois values, as they allowed sons to inherit property and oppressed women by forcing them to do unpaid, low-status labour.

Source E

A propaganda poster entitled 'Moving into a new house'. The poster was produced by the CCP in 1953.

Family life in the towns

The CCP's policies had a significant impact on family life in the cities. Industrialisation led to large numbers of young people migrating to China's cities, which changed family life. In 1949, the majority of Chinese people lived in extended families of several generations living in the same household. However, from 1949 to 1965, there was a rise in the proportion of people living in nuclear families with just parents and their children living together. The rise in nuclear families came about as young people tended to leave their families in the country and move to the cities alone. They would then meet other young people, get married and set up a household in the city, away from the rest of their family.

This trend declined due to the economic chaos of the Great Leap Forward, which meant that lots of jobs in cities were cut, and people returned to the country. Additionally, during the Cultural Revolution, Red Guards tended not to set up nuclear families. Some rejected marriage altogether and experimented with sex outside of marriage. Moreover, during the chaos of the Cultural Revolution, it was difficult to set up stable households.

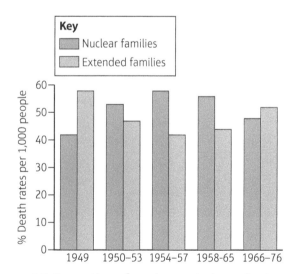

Figure 4.3 Proportion of newly-married couples in cities who set up nuclear families, or lived in extended families.

Family life in the countryside

CCP policies affected family life in the country in a variety of ways. In many rural areas, women made full use of their rights. In some areas, as many as one-quarter of young married couples got divorced, usually because the wife ended the relationship. CCP reports showed that men in rural areas complained of the 'three fears' (see Figure 4.4).

Early land reform helped families. As farming became more efficient, grain supplies improved, rents went down and taxes became fairer, and there was a clear improvement in the standard of living in the countryside.

Interpretation 1

From *A History of China* by Morris Rossabi, published in 2014.

The status of women was still another difficulty that the communists immediately tried to alter. The Marriage Law of 1950 forbade female infanticide, arranged marriages, domestic abuse, and discrimination against women in the labour force. The effects of the law in the early 1950s were decidedly mixed. The government-controlled press acknowledged the persistence of arranged marriages and domestic abuse as late as the 1960s. Communist media also documented unequal wages for women in many enterprises.

The impact of collectivisation

Collectivisation, too, affected families. First, as property was increasingly owned collectively, children tended not to inherit property from their parents. As a result, children in rural areas felt free to move to the cities as there was little financial benefit to staying in the country. Fewer inheritances also meant that young people in rural areas felt less loyal to their parents. As a result, the proportion of nuclear families in the country increased during the 1950s, as couples chose to set up their own households rather than stay with their extended family.

Interpretation 2

From *Mao Zedong's China* by Kathlyn Gay, published in 2007.

Another reform law focused on women and their status within marriage. ... Mao initiated the Marriage Reform Law of 1950, which freed many women from subservient roles. ...

Along with the new marital rights, women obtained new equality under land reform. Previously women had no right to own land, but the Agrarian Reform Law changed that. Men no longer held ownership of all the land. Women were allowed their equal share of the soil that they helped farm. ...

Women worked alongside men in factories and mills.

Fear of not finding
a wife, as women were
becoming too picky.

Fear of being unable
to afford to provide
for a wife.

Fear of being divorced.

Figure 4.4 The 'three fears'.

The impact of the communes

The communes were organised in a way that revolutionised family life:

- Communal canteens were intended to free women from the burden of preparing meals.
- Communal childcare was set up so that women could work on equal terms to men.
- In some communes, men and women were made to live in separate accommodation, and so husbands and wives rarely met each other.

In practice, the CCP's polices failed, resulting in greater hardship for women and families:

- Communal canteens were often miles away from family homes. Therefore, the time saved preparing meals was lost travelling to the canteens.
- Communal childcare was poorly funded and therefore failed to achieve its objectives. Kindergartens were understaffed and held in poorly constructed buildings. Consequently, children were unsupervised and poorly fed. Additionally, diseases such as diarrhoea, chickenpox and measles spread rapidly due to poor sanitation and hygiene. Mothers then had to step in to look after their children.

- After 1959, communal canteens (see Chapter 2.2) provided food according to a system of work points. In practice, men earned more points as they were assigned more demanding jobs. Therefore, women received smaller portions than men.

However, the communes also opened up some opportunities for women. The communes played a key role in the Great Leap Forward, in which women were encouraged to work on equal terms with men in order to boost production. Approximately 90% of women were involved in agricultural production in 1958, compared to only around 70% in 1957. What is more, government propaganda during the Great Leap Forward stressed the importance of female workers in fulfilling the goals of the second Five-Year Plan. In this sense, the Great Leap Forward played a role in increasing the proportion of women who worked and in raising their status.

The impact of the great famine

The great famine led to a major deterioration of family life in rural areas. Starvation led to the re-emergence of female infanticide. Additionally, the burden of feeding children during the famine tended to fall on mothers. Starving women were often exploited by CCP officials. In some cases, women were forced to trade sex for food.

Summary

- Mao was influenced by Chinese feminism and believed that genders would be equal in a socialist society.
- Land reform and the 1950 Marriage Law led to greater independence for women, as they established a legal basis for women's rights.
- While the economy grew, women were encouraged to work on farms and in factories.
- However, the CCP and the economy continued to reflect the traditional pattern, of male dominance.

Checkpoint

Strengthen

S1 Describe two ways in which women were oppressed in traditional Chinese culture.

S2 List three ways in which women's lives improved under the CCP.

S3 List three ways in which CCP policies created inequalities between men and women.

Challenge

C1 Explain why Mao believed that gender equality was an essential part of socialism.

C2 In your own words, evaluate how far conditions for women improved in the period 1949 to 1976.

How confident do you feel about your answers? Have you used evidence in your answers?

4.3 Education and health

- Understand reasons for changes in education under Mao.
- Understand the significance of the growth of literacy and the introduction of Pinyin.
- Understand the reasons for changes in healthcare provision.

The CCP was committed to modernising China by improving healthcare and education. However, education and health had to compete with other priorities for funding. What is more, health and education policies changed over time. Nonetheless, there were significant improvements in health and education between 1949 and 1976.

Source A

A photograph showing a Chinese schoolroom, taken by a Western press photographer in 1950.

Reasons for changes in education

Mao and the CCP believed that China needed an educated workforce to achieve economic growth. In addition, Mao knew that his ideas could be spread more quickly if the population was literate.

Both Mao and the CCP wanted to change education because they were highly critical of traditional education.

First, traditional education had been elitist: it had only been available to the children of the elite, including:

- the children of landlords in rural areas
- the children of factory owners and government officials in towns and cities.

Secondly, communists were critical of the principles that traditional education taught.

- Most education had taught Confucian principles, including a respect for authority (see page 137).
- Additionally, a small number of missionary schools* were founded on Christian principles, which tended to include a respect for imperialism.

As a result of traditional education, there were significant problems in education. In 1949:

- around only 20% of people were literate
- access to schooling was very limited. Only 45% of adult men and 2% of adult women had been given any formal education*.

Mao and the CCP wanted to change education by ending elitism and providing a basic education that reflected the needs of workers and peasants. In the short term, this meant extending literacy.

Key terms

Missionary schools*

Schools established by religious groups based in the West. A missionary is a person sent to promote their religion in another country.

Formal education*

Education that takes place in schools or colleges.

Activities ?

1 Make a bullet point list of the educational problems facing China.

2 Have a class debate about the best ways to solve these problems: agree three key policies to help improve education in China.

3 As you read through the chapter, compare your suggestions to the policies introduced by the CCP to improve education in China.

Growth in literacy

In 1949, the new CCP government was determined to raise the level of literacy. However, there was a series of obstacles in the way of promoting literacy.

- The Chinese spoke a variety of different languages and dialects.
- There was no agreed way of writing Chinese languages.
- Mastering Mandarin, the official language of the People's Republic of China, traditionally meant learning hundreds of different characters.

In order to promote mass literacy, the government introduced Pinyin, a new Mandarin script.

The significance of Pinyin

In 1958, the CCP officially introduced Pinyin, a new written script. Pinyin made learning to read and write easier, because it:

- became the standard script across the whole of China
- reduced the number of characters in the alphabet to around 400, making it easier to learn.

Extend your knowledge

Pinyin

Pinyin is a written script in which each character represents a different sound. In principle, each syllable is represented by a different character. Indeed, the word Pinyin literally means 'spelt out sounds'. Pinyin replaced various types of written language which were based on ideograms, characters which were pictures of the words that they represented.

Educational reform

In addition to Pinyin, the Ministry of Education introduced a series of reforms to promote education and literacy.

- By the end of the 1950s, a national network of primary schools had been established.
- Textbooks were designed to help with the teaching and learning of literacy.
- To support these reforms and to reach adults, literacy drives were launched, backed up by poster campaigns. The drives included the setting up of short-term schools and winter schools for workers and peasants.

Literacy by 1976

Literacy improved greatly due to the introduction of Pinyin and other educational reforms. Literacy rates improved from 20% in 1949 to 50% in 1960 and 70% in 1976. This was a remarkable achievement compared to other developing countries. For example, literacy rates in Kenya and Tanzania, which were ruled by the British Empire until the 1960s, were around 45% in 1976.

The collapse of education after 1966

The Cultural Revolution had a devastating short-term effect on education. During 1966, education at China's universities and the majority of middle schools* stopped completely, disrupting the education of around 130 million students. From 1968, the 'Up to the mountains and down to the villages' campaign effectively ended the formal education of around 100 million Chinese young people who became known as the 'lost generation'.

The Cultural Revolution also had an impact on primary education. Jiang Qing gave orders to destroy textbooks produced before 1966. New textbooks were commissioned, but they focused on praising Mao's thoughts rather than on literacy or other kinds of learning.

Key term

Middle school*

A school which provided education for students aged between 12 and 15.

Source B

A poster published by the CCP in 1969, during the 'Up to the mountains and down to the villages' campaign. The poster is entitled 'Educated youth must go to the countryside to receive re-education from the poor and lower-middle peasants!'

THINKING HISTORICALLY Interpretations (2b)

The importance of perspective

What we notice when we look at a historical source is shaped by our interests, questions and concepts. Historians are individuals too, and what they 'see' is shaped by what they are interested in and what they see as important. Historians also sometimes use different methods of investigating and will make sense of sources in different ways.

Study Source B and the information about it.

The poster shows 'traces' of the past (e.g. the copies of the 'Little Red Book'). Traces can be interpreted in many ways, depending on the questions asked and the interests and concepts that we bring to them.

1 Look closely at the poster and the accompanying text. Discuss the following questions with a partner and write down your ideas.

   a What might a **cultural historian** notice about the picture? What story would they tell about the themes of CCP propaganda?

   b What might a **political historian** with an interest in how the CCP controlled the Chinese people notice? What story might they tell about the methods of control used by the CCP?

   c Explain how the two stories differ and why.

2 Sometimes historians look at history in great depth, but sometimes they are interested in getting more of an overview of what happened. Look at the image again.

   a How would a historian interested in education in the whole of Asia study this poster? How much detail would they go into, and what might they compare it to?

   b How would a historian interested in education in China's villages study this poster? How much detail would they go into, and what might they compare it to?

   c Explain how the **scale** that a historian is thinking about affects how they look at sources.

3 Answer the following question in a paragraph of your own: How important are the interests, questions and concepts that historians bring to their study of the past in shaping their interpretations?

Source C

From a letter to Mao Zedong written by Li Qinglin in 1973. Mao responded, sending Li money to help his son aid the villagers he was working with.

Esteemed Chairman Mao:

I sincerely wish you longevity (ten thousand years' long life). ...

I am a teacher at the Putian Primary School, Putian County, Fujian Province. Ever since Liberation [1949] I have busied myself in the Party's educational work, and have always been keen in participating in all past campaigns.

Your policy of 'young intellectuals going to receive education from the poor and lower-middle peasants' was correct, and I wholeheartedly support it. In response, my son went without hesitation to a distant hilly area to receive his re-education.

Exam-style question, Section A

Give two things you can infer from Source C about education in China after 1966. **4 marks**

Exam tip

You infer something from a source by working out something the source does not actually tell you directly. In this case, think about how the writer describes his work since 1949.

However, in the longer term, the Cultural Revolution led to important educational reforms. From 1969, education became more egalitarian. The CCP introduced:

- more rural primary schools
- new adult literacy schemes
- greater access to middle schools and universities for the children of peasants and working people.

These reforms significantly improved access to education and literacy rates.

Source D

From a memoir of Ye Weili, a student during the Cultural Revolution. Her friend Ma joined the Red Guards in 1966.

At the beginning of the Cultural Revolution in the summer of 1966, many people in my age group eagerly responded to Chairman Mao's call, 'It's right to rebel.' ... In my school female students beat a school leader to death. Ma Xiaodong [her best friend] participated in beating an alleged class enemy on her school campus, only to find a few days later that her own mother, leader of a secondary school, suffered severe physical abuse at the hands of her students.

Source E

From Fan Shen's memoir, published in 1996. Fan was 12 years old at the beginning of the Cultural Revolution and quickly joined the Red Guards.

On September 1 [1966], I went to school to see if it would open as it had in previous years and I found out quickly — even without reading the notice at the gate — that the school would not open this year. In fact, most of the teachers and school officials were gone. Some, like my math teacher ... had been arrested by the Red Guards as anti-revolutionaries and had been locked up in the basement of the school. Others, the 'problem-free' ones, had joined the Red Guards ...

Exam-style question, Section B

How useful are Sources D and E for an enquiry into the impact of the Cultural Revolution on education? Explain your answer, using Sources D and E and your knowledge of the historical context.

8 marks

Exam tip

When considering how useful sources are, be sure to focus on the subject of the enquiry. Consider what aspects of the enquiry the sources discuss, and if there are important aspects they leave out.

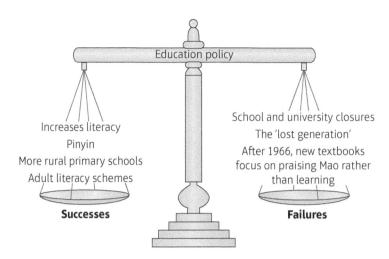

Figure 4.5 The impact of the CCP's educational policy.

Changes in healthcare

In 1949, access to healthcare was extremely limited for the vast majority of the population, especially for those in remote areas. Missionaries and Western charities had established hospitals that offered Western medicine. However, there were very few of these, and almost none outside the major cities.

The CCP's commitment to equality included a determination to make healthcare available to all. However, this was extremely difficult as healthcare was expensive. Consequently, the CCP introduced a series of pragmatic measures designed to offer basic medical treatment to as many people as possible.

The significance of barefoot doctors

Barefoot doctors were the CCP's solution to providing healthcare for peasants. Barefoot doctors were first introduced in 1949. In 1965, there were around a quarter of a million barefoot doctors; by 1970, as a result of Mao's reforms during the Cultural Revolution, there were around 1 million.

In essence, the CCP organised basic medical training for better educated peasants, so that they could offer simple medical care to other peasants. Barefoot doctors were trained:

- in hygiene, in order to prevent the occurrence of some diseases and the spread of disease
- in family planning* techniques
- to spot and offer remedies for common illnesses
- to administer vaccines*.

Key terms

Family planning*

Advice on how to control the number of children conceived.

Vaccines*

Medicine that makes people immune to certain diseases.

Source F

A photograph published by the CCP in 1972, showing a barefoot doctor meeting patients in Inner Mongolia.

Patriotic health movements

The hygiene work carried out by the early barefoot doctors was backed by health campaigns called patriotic health movements. These emphasised the link between dirt and disease, and the need for good sanitation*.

The CCP produced large picture posters warning about the causes of diseases. For example, the campaigns encouraged peasants to dispose of human waste in a way that did not contaminate food or crops, to use nets to protect food from contamination by insects, and to keep rats out of villages.

Interpretation 1

From *China's Sent-Down Generation* by Helena K. Rene, published in 2013.

The Great Leap Forward ended in an unprecedented disaster …

The cost of stabilisation was an increasing disparity [inequality] between the urban and rural populations and especially between the technocrats and the rest of the society. … Medical care in the rural areas drastically declined as economic resources were shifted back to the urban sectors. As the gap between urban and rural health care grew, Mao complained that China's healthcare system should be renamed the 'Ministry of Urban Gentlemen's Health'.

Interpretation 2

From *Governing Health in Contemporary China* by Yanzhong Huang, published in 2015.

By 1976, 1.8 million barefoot doctors were trained … China came to have more professional doctors, nurses, and hospital beds than virtually any country near its level of economic development. This represents a monumental achievement because many more people had access to some level of healthcare than ever before. As a result, the health status of the Chinese people improved remarkably … To many Chinese, the years between 1965 and 1976 were the golden days of healthcare.

Medical provision

As the economy improved in the 1950s and again in the 1960s, the CCP invested in healthcare.

- Each commune contained a medical clinic in order to serve the local peasants.
- CCP training produced over 100,000 fully qualified doctors between 1949 and 1965.
- By 1965, medical schools were training 25,000 medical doctors a year.
- During the 1950s and 1960s, the CCP built more than 800 modern hospitals.

Key term

Sanitation*

The disposal of waste and the provision of clean drinking water.

Activities

1 In groups, decide how useful Sources A, B and F are for an enquiry into the impact of CCP health and education policies in the years 1949–76. Select two sources which, together, are the most useful.

2 Compare the list your group has made with another group. Are they different?

3 Write a short paragraph to explain why your group chose those particular sources.

Exam-style question, Section B

Study Interpretations 1 and 2. They give different views about the success of CCP healthcare policies. What is the main difference between these views?

Explain your answer, using details from both interpretations.

4 marks

Exam tip

When answering a question about how interpretations differ, be sure to quote details from both interpretations to support what you say, or you will lose marks.

Exam-style question, Section B

How far do you agree with Interpretation 1 about the success of CCP healthcare policies? Explain your answer, using Interpretations 1 and 2 and your knowledge of the historical context.   **16 marks**

Exam tip

When answering a question of this kind, use knowledge of the historical context to support and challenge the views given in the interpretations.

The successes and failures of healthcare reform

Medical policy was extremely effective. Between 1950 and 1965, China's medical system expanded at a faster rate than in any other country in history. As a result of vaccinations, cholera, plague and smallpox were eradicated. Educational campaigns also meant that sexually transmitted diseases and opium addiction were wiped out by 1965.

Mao's policy of ensuring that healthcare was available in rural areas was also effective. By 1976, 85% of the rural population had access to a doctor, and every commune had a clinic. China's healthcare system was better than that of any other developing nation. As a result, the overall mortality rate dropped from 20 per 1,000 in 1949 to 7 per 1,000 in 1976, and infant mortality fell, too. Life expectancy rose from 36 to 66 years in the same period.

However, there were problems with the Chinese healthcare system. First, people in rural areas rarely had access to expensive drugs. Secondly, there were still less than 2 million hospital beds to serve a population of more than 900 million people. Finally, Party officials tended to receive better treatment than most citizens.

Activity ?

Using the information in Chapters 2 and 4, hold a debate on the statement: 'Communist rule greatly benefited China's workers and peasants'.

Summary

- Improving healthcare and education were key goals of the CCP in 1949.
- Educational reforms introduced from the early 1950s succeeded in raising literacy levels.
- Healthcare reforms succeeded in improving hygiene and vaccinating people against common diseases.
- In the short term, the Cultural Revolution led to a huge disruption of education in urban areas.
- In the longer term, the Cultural Revolution led to more egalitarian health and education policies.

Checkpoint

Strengthen

S1 Describe two of the CCP's goals for healthcare in China.

S2 Describe two of the CCP's goals for education in China.

S3 Outline the different policies the CCP introduced to improve healthcare and education in China.

Challenge

C1 In no more than 40 words, evaluate how far CCP reforms met their aims in education.

C2 In your own words, evaluate how far CCP healthcare reforms met their aims.

C3 Write a summary of the Cultural Revolution's impact on education.

How confident do you feel about your answers to these questions? If you're not sure you have answered them well, try writing thought bubbles about how Chinese students might feel about education and how a Chinese family might feel about changes in healthcare.

4.4 Cultural change

Learning outcomes

- Understand the reasons why the CCP attacked traditional culture.
- Understand Jiang Qing's role in the development of revolutionary art and culture.
- Understand the CCP's imposition of revolutionary culture.
- Understand the reasons for the CCP's attacks on religion.

Reasons for attacks on traditional culture

Mao believed that culture had a political role. For Mao, traditional culture and Western culture prevented people from thinking like communists. Mao believed that a series of revolutions were necessary to create a socialist society, as shown in Figure 4.6. Therefore, he was keen to purge culture and to use the arts to gain support for the CCP.

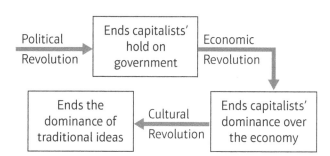

Figure 4.6 Mao's view of revolutions.

Destroying traditional culture was an essential part of the CCP's programme. However, the attack on traditional culture impacted the towns and the countryside differently.

- In rural areas, the Confucian* religion was the foundation of the property system. Therefore, land reform was accompanied by a cultural war against landlords and the Confucian religion.
- In the towns, the CCP attacked examples of bourgeois culture, which it claimed promoted selfish behaviour.

Key term

Confucianism*

A traditional Chinese system of ethics and philosophy based on the teachings of Confucius (c.551–c.479 BC). It was a cornerstone of Chinese culture for thousands of years.

Cultural reform in the countryside

In 1950, CCP leaders created a 'cultural army' of Red Drama Groups to tour rural areas and win over the peasants in newly captured areas. Red Drama Groups were involved in a variety of activities to support CCP policy, including:

- performing radical plays, operas and ballets
- encouraging peasants to take action
- writing new plays about the experience of land reform.

The White-haired Girl is an example of a play promoting land reform, which was performed in the late 1940s and early 1950s. *The White-haired Girl*, which tells the story of a group of peasants who rebel against a landlord, drew huge crowds in rural areas, encouraging peasants to seize land.

Source A

A photograph of a performance by a Red Drama Group in Hubei Province, central China in 1959.

Cultural reform in the towns

The CCP attempted to reform urban culture during the early 1950s. For example, theatre directors were physically attacked during the thought control campaign of 1951, and theatre owners were targeted during the 'antis' movements. As a result, some aspects of urban culture changed. For example, Shanxi opera, a traditional form of opera, was reformed in the following ways:

- Overtly sexual themes were criticised as obscene, and therefore removed from performances.
- Working-class characters were rewritten to make them heroic.
- Stupid or devious working-class characters were dropped from plays, ballets and operas.
- Directors no longer required peasant characters to wear fierce masks.
- Music was made quieter so that audiences could hear all of the words.

Confronting Western ideas

During the Cultural Revolution, Mao emphasised that Chinese people needed to reject Western ideas. Mao argued that Western ideas particularly affected cities where standards of living were higher. In essence, Mao argued that selfishness and individualism were two dangerous Western ideas because they encouraged people to focus on their own needs, rather than on the need to build a communist society for the good of all.

In practice, confronting Western ideas included:

- attacking young people, particularly young women, who wore Western clothes, hairstyles or makeup
- attacking people who listened to Western music, or read Western books.

Source B

From the magazine *People's China*, published in 1951. *People's China* was published by the CCP to win foreign support.

In *Gate No. 6*, hailed by the public and critics as the best workers' play of 1950, you see how the Chinese transport workers lived and toiled in hell and how they won their way to freedom. It is a story of real life — but life artistically concentrated — that has taken its place on the stage. ...

In August, 1950, the play was first presented to the public in Tientsin's Cultural Palace for Workers. Its success was immediate. The audience was extraordinarily moved. Transport workers after seeing it commented: 'Not one note [aspect of the play] is false. These words are taken from our own hearts.'

THINKING HISTORICALLY — Evidence (3b)

It depends on the question

When considering the usefulness of historical sources, people often consider 'reliability' (whether a witness can be trusted). This is important; however, some sources are not witnesses – they are simply the remains of the past.

Work in small groups.

1 Imagine you are investigating how far drama created support for the CCP in the period 1949–57. Look at Source A.

   a Write at least two statements that you can reasonably infer about how far drama created support for the CCP in the period 1949–57, based solely on Source A.

   b Which of your statements are you most sure of? Explain your answer.

2 Source B is unreliable testimony – its author had good reason not to tell the truth. Try to think of at least two statements that you can still reasonably infer about how far drama created support for the CCP in the period 1949–57 using this source.

3 Which source is more useful for investigating how far drama created support for the CCP in the period 1949–57? Explain your answer.

4 In your group, discuss the following question and write down your thoughts: How are reliability and usefulness related?

The role of Jiang Qing

During the Cultural Revolution, Mao appointed Jiang Qing as 'cultural purifier of the nation', instructing her to purge traditional ideas from Chinese culture. She was part of the Cultural Revolution Group that ordered attacks on the 'four olds' (see page 87). She also played a key role in the production of model plays which were designed to show what truly revolutionary culture should look like (see page 133).

Jiang's motives

Jiang had several motives for her role in Chinese culture during the 1960s.

- She had been an actress in her youth, and was therefore knowledgeable about theatre.
- She was a radical and therefore ideologically committed to purging old, anti-communist values from Chinese culture.
- She was also a politician who wanted to build a powerbase within the government.
- She had enemies within the government and within Chinese theatre, and she was willing to persecute them using her official power.

Source C

A poster showing Jiang Qing holding a copy of the 'Little Red Book'. The poster was published in 1967 by the Worker-peasant-soldier Illustrated Editorial Group, a group of radical communists.

向江青同志学习 向江青同志致敬

The imposition of revolutionary art and culture

In the early stages of the Cultural Revolution, Jiang took firm control of the censorship of all forms of art. She began purging culture by banning performances of virtually all plays, ballets and operas being staged in China. Jiang repeated Mao's declaration that artists should be the servants of the people, meaning that their work should inspire and educate the population. She demanded works of art that represented modern revolutionary themes, not traditional ideas and stories – with workers, peasants and soldiers as the heroes. She said art should be 'red, bright and shining'.

Professional artists were no longer free to create their own work, unless commissioned by the government. Instead, trained artists were sent to the countryside for re-education, to teach and learn from peasants.

Source D

From a speech made by Jiang Qing at a CCP forum on theatre, during the Festival of Beijing Opera. The speech was made in July 1964.

It is inconceivable [unthinkable] that, in our socialist country led by the Communist Party, the dominant position on the stage is not occupied by the workers, peasants and soldiers, who are the real creators of history and the true masters of our country. We should create literature and art which protect our socialist economic base. ...

We should place the emphasis on creating artistic images of advanced revolutionaries so as to educate and inspire the people and lead them forward.

Exam-style question, Section A

Give two things you can infer from Source D about Jiang Qing's motives for reforming Chinese culture.

4 marks

Exam tip

You infer something from a source by working out something the source does not actually tell you directly. In this case, consider Jiang's proposals for changing Chinese culture.

Jiang quickly commissioned eight operas and two ballets to model the radical art that she wanted to create. These included:

- *Taking Tiger Mountain, by Strategy* celebrates a heroic victory by PLA soldiers during the Civil War.
- *Red Detachment of Women* celebrates an all-female PLA platoon that destroyed a nationalist base during the Civil War.

However, the Cultural Revolution failed to generate a whole new culture. The majority of China's artists stopped producing work for fear of being denounced as 'capitalist roaders' by Jiang. With the exception of the few plays that Jiang approved, very little new culture was produced during the Cultural Revolution.

Activity ?

Imagine you are part of a Red Drama Group. Write a short (three-minute) play, designed to promote an aspect of CCP policy. You should have a minimum of four characters and a clear political message.

Source E

A photograph of a scene from the revolutionary ballet *Red Detachment of Women*. The image appeared on a series of postcards advertising the ballet, published by the CCP in 1970.

Reasons for attacks on religion

Religious worship was widespread in China before 1949. Most members of the CCP argued that religious beliefs were based on ignorance. Therefore, religions would die out over time as people gained a better education and understanding of science. Nonetheless, the CCP was suspicious of religions such as Confucianism and Christianity, which they believed justified inequality. Also, religious leaders were an alternative source of beliefs and authority to the CCP.

Article 88 of the Chinese constitution of 1954 officially established freedom of conscience*. However, in practice the government ignored constitutional rights and persecuted the major religious groups in China.

Key term

Freedom of conscience*
The right to follow any religion or no religion.

Attacking Buddhism

Buddhism was one of China's major religions in 1949. The CCP attacked Buddhism as part of an invasion of Tibet in 1950. CCP leaders recognised that Buddhism was a crucial part of Tibetan culture and were concerned that Buddhists might organise resistance to Chinese rule. Following Chinese victory in Tibet in 1950, Lamaism, the Tibetan form of Buddhism, was banned.

The CCP accused Buddhist priests of being parasites – that is to say, they accused them of refusing to work and living off the hard work of others. Buddhism was repeatedly attacked by the CCP.

- The suppression of Buddhism intensified during the Resist America, Aid Korea campaign, during which the CCP converted Buddhist temples into barracks and hospitals for soldiers involved in the war.
- It was attacked during the 'Anti-Rightist' purge and the 'four olds' campaign. During the 'four olds' campaign, temples, statues of Buddha and religious items were destroyed and Buddhist monks and nuns were killed, beaten or sent to labour camps.

Although attacks on Buddhism helped the CCP to conquer Tibet, they failed to destroy the religion. Indeed, from the mid-1970s, Buddhists across China began to restore the damage done to their temples.

Attacking Confucianism

In 1949, Confucianism was very influential in China. Confucianism is a philosophy based on the writing of the Chinese thinker Confucius. Confucian philosophy – such as *san gang*, the 'Three Guiding Principles' – stressed the importance of respecting traditional authority and therefore was considered dangerous by the CCP.

As soon as the PRC was established, the CCP banned major festivals that celebrated Confucius. Temples and shrines were also closed. Propaganda blamed Confucianism for the oppression of women and peasants, because of its emphasis on the authority of men and landlords.

Confucianism came under even more vigorous attack during the Cultural Revolution. During the 'four olds' campaign, Red Guards destroyed Confucian temples and shrines, including the temple at Confucius's birthplace. Confucianism was attacked again as part of a 'Criticise Lin Biao and Criticise Confucius' campaign, which accused Lin of being influenced by Confucianism.

Attacking Christianity

The CCP believed that Christianity had been brought to China by European capitalists, and was part of their plan to dominate China. The CCP opposed the Roman Catholic Church* and Protestant* forms of Christianity.

The Protestant church

Between 1951 and 1954, the CCP's Religious Affairs Department forced Western Protestant missionaries to leave China. The CCP also took over hospitals, schools and universities that had been set up by Christian missionaries. The Religious Affairs Department was extremely successful, as almost all of the 3,000 Protestant missionaries who had been in China in 1949 had been expelled by mid-1952.

Source F

A photograph published in Germany in a national newspaper in 1967. It shows a Red Guard destroying a Confucian temple during the Cultural Revolution.

Key terms

Roman Catholic Church*
A Christian organisation headed by the Pope.

Protestant*
A form of Christianity which emerged in the sixteenth century and which rejects some aspects of Roman Catholic teachings.

Chinese Protestants were encouraged to join the Patriotic Three-Self Church, which was established by the CCP in 1951 and allowed Protestants to continue to practise some aspects of their faith. Many Protestants refused to join the official church because the CCP limited its activities. Consequently, a secret house church movement* emerged in the mid-1950s. The CCP responded by imprisoning leaders of house churches. For example, Pastor Samuel Lamb, a Chinese Christian leader, was imprisoned in a labour camp for 20 years for setting up a church in the city of Guangzhou. Lamb, originally known as Lin Xiangao, had changed his name to reflect his religious beliefs.

The Patriotic Three-Self Church was banned during the Cultural Revolution. This led to the growth of the house church movement, which grew from around 200,000 in the 1940s to several million by 1976.

Key term

House church movement*

Christian churches which met in the houses of church members, rather than in traditional church buildings.

Extend your knowledge

The Patriotic Three-Self Church

The Patriotic Three-Self Church was established as the official Protestant church in China in 1951. From 1951 to 1966, it followed the 'three-self-principle' of being self-governing, self-funding and recruiting its own members. In reality, the CCP set important limits on the church. For example, the Patriotic Three-Self Church could not openly discuss issues related to the end of the world or parts of the Bible that referred to Jesus returning to Earth.

The Roman Catholic Church

After 1949, Roman Catholic missionaries were also forced to leave China: all but 364 of the original 3,222 Catholic missionaries were forced out by 1953. The CCP launched a propaganda campaign against the Roman Catholic Church which accused Catholic missionaries of murdering and exploiting children. The CCP also closed many Catholic churches and took over Catholic schools and hospitals in the early 1950s.

When the Patriotic Three-Self Church was established, Catholic clergymen were encouraged to join. However, the Pope, the head of the Roman Catholic Church, threatened to excommunicate any clergymen appointed by the Chinese government. Excommunication is the most serious penalty the Roman Catholic Church can inflict, and cuts off a person from any involvement in the Church.

All remaining Catholic churches were closed during the Cultural Revolution. However, estimates suggest that CCP policy against the Catholic Church had little impact. Indeed, there were around 3 million Catholics in China in 1949 and around the same number in 1976.

Interpretation 1

From *The People's Republic of China 1949–76* by Michael Lynch, published in 2008.

Almost immediately after the Chinese Communists came to power, the attack on religion began. The officially stated justification was since the workers were now in power there was no longer any reason for religion to exist; the triumph of the workers had ended the need for such escapism. For religion to continue openly would be an affront to the new Chinese Communist world. The authorities would not tolerate the people's continuing adherence to a corrupt thought process. Religious worship had now to be replaced by loyalty to the Communist Party and the state.

Activities ?

1. Read Interpretation 1 and write a summary of its key argument about CCP policy towards religion in 20 words or less.
2. Using an internet search engine or your school's learning resource centre, search for an interpretation which gives an alternative point of view.
3. Copy down a passage giving an alternative point of view, and write an exam-style question on the CCP's approach to religion.

Attacking Islam

Muslims*, too, were persecuted by the CCP. Their religion, Islam*, represented a rival set of values to communism, and the local mosques and religious leaders, imams, had the authority to challenge communism within their communities. The CCP was also worried about where Muslims were located. The majority of Chinese Muslims lived in regions along China's northwestern border. The CCP was concerned that Chinese Muslims could break away from China and join the nearby states in which Muslims formed the majority of the population.

The PLA targeted the northwest border region in an attempt to crush Islamic resistance to communist rule. As with other religions, attacks on Islam involved confiscating property and establishing an official association in order to impose government control over the Muslims. Islamic schools were also closed and Muslim children were forced to attend government-run schools in which the Islamic values and culture were not taught.

Muslims were attacked viciously during the Cultural Revolution. Mosques were defiled* by turning them into slaughterhouses for pigs, which, according to Islamic law, Muslims are forbidden from eating. Muslim leaders were forced to breed pigs and eat pork. Muslims in the northwest of China were forced to abandon their traditional clothes, which were associated with their faith, and wear the costumes of Red Guards.

Attacking ancestor worship

In 1949, ancestor worship, the traditional practice of paying respect to the ghosts and spirits of dead relatives, was widespread. The CCP attacked ancestor worship because communists believed it was a superstitious tradition which kept people trapped in traditional ways of thinking. Traditionally, at New Year, Chinese people would return to their family home to celebrate their ancestors and make smaller offerings to the Kitchen Gods*. The CCP did not discourage celebrating New Year, or returning home. However, they started a campaign to encourage people to end 'superstitious' customs, such as making offerings to the Kitchen Gods.

Controlling ancestor worship was easier once the communes had been introduced. Indeed, the communes tended to break the link between people and their family homes, as no one within the communes owned property. Nonetheless, traditional customs associated with ancestor worship continued. Indeed, following his death in 1976, millions of peasants began to worship Mao in the same way they worshipped their ancestors.

Exam-style question, Section A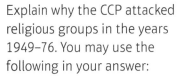

Explain why the CCP attacked religious groups in the years 1949–76. You may use the following in your answer:

- the invasion of Tibet in 1950
- the 'four olds' campaign.

You **must** also use information of your own. **12 marks**

Exam tip

When answering a question like this, it is a good idea to talk about the bullet point items in your answer. However, to get the top marks you must also add a point of your own to support your answer.

Activities **?**

1 Make a table with five columns, headed 'Buddhism', 'Confucianism', 'Christianity', 'Islam' and 'ancestor worship'.

2 In each column, list the ways in which the CCP tackled these different beliefs.

3 In a class discussion, evaluate how effectively the CCP challenged religious beliefs in the years to 1976.

Conclusion

Despite the Chinese constitution, the CCP persecuted religions and traditional beliefs. However, persecution largely failed and, in some cases, as religious groups went underground, they flourished.

Summary

- Mao and leading members of the CCP believed that traditional Chinese culture contained values that were obstacles to socialism.
- The CCP used drama to inspire peasants to embrace land reform.
- Jiang Qing played a key role in commissioning new revolutionary opera and ballet to exemplify the new revolutionary culture she wanted China to develop.
- CCP leaders believed that religion and the authority of religious leaders was an obstacle to the establishment of socialism in China.

Checkpoint

Strengthen

S1 Outline two problems with traditional culture identified by Mao and CCP leaders.

S2 Outline two ways in which Jiang Qing attempted to transform Chinese culture.

S3 Outline the different methods used by the CCP and the PLA to crush religious groups in the years 1949–58.

Challenge

C1 In your own words, evaluate how far Jiang Qing achieved her aims of reforming culture by 1976.

C2 In your own words, evaluate how far the CCP and PLA campaigns against religious groups met the CCP's aims in the period 1949–76.

How confident do you feel about your answers to these questions? If you are not sure that you answered them well, discuss the answers with a group of other students, and then record your conclusions.

Recap: Life in Mao's China, 1949–76

Recall quiz

1 Why did the CCP launch a campaign against Hu Feng in 1955?
2 How many people died in *Laogai* camps between 1949 and 1976?
3 List three customs banned by the Marriage Law of 1950.
4 Define androgynous.
5 List three consequences of CCP rule on family life in China.
6 By what percentage did literacy rates increase in China from 1949 to 1976?
7 Explain three ways in which barefoot doctors improved healthcare in China.
8 Explain why Jiang Qing wanted to reform Chinese culture – list three reasons.
9 What was the name of the official Protestant church in China from 1951 to 1966?
10 List three ways in which the CCP persecuted religious groups in the 1950s.

Activities ?

1 On a large sheet of paper, draw a timeline of the period 1949 to 1976.
2 Mark in the major events, including collectivisation and the Cultural Revolution.
3 Using your notes from this section, add information to your timeline dealing with:
   • propaganda and censorship
   • thought control and the *Laogai* system
   • family life
   • the role and status of women
   • education policy
   • health policy
   • cultural policy
   • attacks on religion.
You should use different colours for each aspect of communist rule.

Exam-style question, Section B

Study Sources B and D (on pages 134 and 135).

How useful are the sources for an enquiry into the impact of drama on support for the CCP in the period 1949–57? Explain your answer, using Sources B and D and your knowledge of the historical context. **8 marks**

Exam tip

When considering how useful sources are, remember to take into account three things: content, provenance and context. Consider the information the sources provide and think about how the purpose or origin of the source might affect its usefulness. Don't forget to consider the historical context.

Explaining why historians' interpretations differ

In Paper 3, one question will ask you to suggest one reason why two interpretations give different views about an aspect of your study. To understand the reasons for difference you need to appreciate that historians writing about any society have to make choices and they have to make judgements. They choose what to concentrate on. They also come to views about the topics they research. Historians may be focusing on different aspects, using different sources, or reaching different conclusions on the same sources. These factors explain reasons for difference.

Historians focus on different things

Interpretations of history are created by historians. Historians construct interpretations based on evidence from the past. Think of their role as similar to a house-builder: the evidence – the sources available – are the building blocks for their construction. Historians choose what enquiries to make of the materials available to them. No historian can write about the whole of history everywhere. What shapes the historian's work is what they want to explore and what they choose to focus on. Figure 1 below lists some of the choices they make:

Place	National history	Local history
Period	One century or more	One decade or less
Range	Overview	Depth
People	National leaders	Ordinary people
Aspect	Political history	Social history

Figure 1 Some examples of historians' choices.

Figure 2 The historian's focus.

After choosing their focus, the historian must find evidence to pursue their enquiry. So, they will be looking for different things in order to answer different questions about the past.

Historians A and B below are both writing about the same school, but their focus is different. In looking at the history of a school, several different enquiries are possible, for example the focus could be on the building, the curriculum, students' achievements and so on. As you read the interpretations below, identify what the two historians are interested in – what have their enquiries focused on?

Historian A

The village school has been in continuous use since 1870. It continues to educate local children from the ages of 5-11. They are educated in the same building that was constructed in 1870. Its outward appearance has hardly changed. It was originally built of red brick, with white-painted wooden doors and the large windows that can still be seen today. The schoolroom windows, reaching almost to the high ceiling, were designed to give plenty of light, but with windowsills too high for students to be distracted by being able to see anything outside. Although a modern extension at the rear was added in the 1960s, the key features of the school building represent a remarkable degree of continuity in education in the locality.

Historian B

Education locally has changed in the period since 1870. Lessons in the 19th century focused almost entirely on the 3Rs of reading, writing and arithmetic. There was much learning by heart and copying out of passages. By the 21st century, the wall displays and the students' exercise books show that science, history, geography, have all become important parts of the curriculum and with more emphasis on finding out and creativity. In terms of the curriculum, the degree of change in education since 1870 has been considerable.

Read each of the statements about Historians A and B below.

a The historians have different views about the amount of change in education in the village.

b One of the historians is wrong.

c One of the historians is biased.

d They are just giving different opinions.

e They have used different evidence.

f They have focused on different aspects.

g They are both correct in their conclusions.

h They have emphasised different things.

i They are looking for different things.

j The historians disagree.

k The historians do not disagree.

1 Make a list of each of the statements you agree with and another list of those that you do not agree with.

2 Explain why Historians A and B have different views about the extent to which education has changed in the village. Try to use words from the box below in your answer:

| focus | emphasis | aspect | evidence | conclusions | enquiry | interested |

Historians reach different conclusions from the evidence

Even when historians have the same focus and purpose – for example, even if they both seek to explain why the same thing happened – their conclusions may still be different. This is because the evidence from the past doesn't provide us with an answer: historians have to work out an answer from it – and often the evidence points in different directions. Then, the historians have to make judgements. Differences may arise because:

- they have given weight to different sources
- they have reached different conclusions on the same sources.

In a court of law, every member of the jury hears the same evidence, but they sometimes disagree about their verdict. It comes down to making judgements about what conclusions can be drawn from the evidence.

Study Interpretations 1 and 2 on page 56.

Which of the following reasons explains why the views in Interpretations 1 and 2 are different? Make a list of all those that you think apply. You can add other reasons of your own if you wish.

a The historians are interested in different aspects of the topic.

b The historians have emphasised different things when giving their views.

c The evidence from the period points in different directions.

d The historians have reached conclusions by giving weight to different sources from the period.

Choose one reason you have listed and write one or two sentences to explain why you chose it. Remember to use the interpretations in your answer. Refer to sources from the period too, if you listed reason c or d.

- What shapes the historian's work is which aspect of history the historian chooses to explore.
- Historians' judgements differ because the evidence can support different views. They may reach different conclusions because they have given weight to different sources or because they are looking at different aspects of the topic.

Preparing for your GCSE Paper 3 exam

Paper 3 overview

Your Paper 3 is in two sections that examine the Modern Depth Study. In Section A you answer a question on a source and one using your own knowledge. Section B is a case study using sources and interpretations of history, and the four questions will be about the same issue. The paper is worth 30% of your History assessment.

History Paper 3	Modern Depth Study		Time 1 hour 20 minutes
Section A	Answer 2 questions	16 marks	20 minutes
Section B	Answer 4 questions	32 marks + 4 for SPaG	60 minutes

Modern Depth Option 32: Mao's China, 1945–76

Section A

You will answer Questions 1 and 2.

1 Give two things you can infer from Source A about... (4 marks)

Source A is on the question paper. You should work out two inferences from it. An inference is something not directly stated in the source, but which you can support using details from it.

You have a table to complete for each inference: 'What I can infer…' and 'Details in the source that tell me this'. Allow 5 minutes to read the source and to write your answer. This question is only worth 4 marks and you should keep the answer brief and not try to put more information on extra lines.

2 Explain why... (12 marks)

This question asks you to explain the reasons why something happened. Allow 15 minutes to write your answer. You are given two information points as prompts to help you. You do not have to use the prompts and you will not lose marks by leaving them out. Always remember to add in a new point of your own as well: higher marks are gained by adding in a point extra to the prompts. You will be given at least

two pages of lines in the answer booklet for your answer. This does not mean you should try to fill all the space. The front page of the exam paper tells you 'there may be more space than you need'. Aim to write an answer giving at least three explained reasons.

Section B

You will answer Question 3 (a), (b), (c) and (d). All four questions will be about the same issue. Question (a) will be based on contemporary sources (evidence from the period you are studying). Questions (b), (c) and (d) will be based on two historical interpretations.

3(a) How useful are Sources B and C for an enquiry into... (8 marks)

You are given two sources to evaluate. They are in a separate sources booklet so you can keep them in front of you while you write your answer. Allow 15 minutes for this question to give yourself time to read both sources carefully. Make sure your answer deals with both sources and use your knowledge when you evaluate the source. You could use it, for example, to evaluate the accuracy or completeness of the evidence. You should make a judgement about the usefulness of each source, giving clear reasons. Only choose points which are directly relevant to the enquiry in the question. You should always take account of the provenance (the nature, origin and purpose) of the source when you think about the usefulness of the information it gives. How reliable is it?

3(b) Study Interpretations 1 and 2. They give different views about...

What is the main difference between these views? (4 marks)

Allow 10 minutes for this question to give yourself time to read the extracts. Identify an **overall** difference rather than different pieces of information. For example, think about whether one is positive and the other negative. Then use details from both. *The difference is… this is shown because Interpretation 1 says… but Interpretation 2 says…*

3(c) Suggest one reason why Interpretations 1 and 2 give different views about... (4 marks)

Allow 5 minutes for this question. It does not need a long answer (it is only worth 4 marks) and you have already read the interpretations, but you will need to use both the extracts again and perhaps Sources B and C. Give a clear reason for the difference. This could be because the historians have chosen to give weight to different evidence. If you use this reason, you should use Sources B and C to show that the evidence from the period differs.

3(d) How far do you agree with Interpretation [1 or 2] about... ? (16 marks + 4 marks SPaG)

This question, including SPaG, is worth 20 marks – over one-third of your marks for the whole of the Modern Depth Study. Make sure you have kept 30 minutes of the exam time to answer it and to check your spelling, punctuation and grammar. You will already have worked out the views in the two interpretations for Question (b). Question (d) asks you how far you agree with the view in one of them. Plan your answer before you begin to write, and put your points in two columns:

For and Against. You should use points from the two interpretations and also use your own contextual knowledge. Think about it as if you were putting weight on each side to decide what your judgement is going to be for the conclusion. That way your whole answer hangs together – it is coherent. Be clear about your reasons (your criteria) for your judgement.

In this question, 4 extra marks will be gained for good spelling, punctuation and grammar. Use sentences, paragraphs, capital letters, commas and full stops, etc. Try also to use relevant specialist terms – for example, terms such as constitution, communism, collectivisation.

For

Points from the interpretation linked to

points from own knowledge

Against

Points from the other interpretation linked to

points from own knowledge

Conclusion

Paper 3, Section A: Question 1

Study Source B on page 79.
Give **two** things you can infer from Source B about the CCP in the early 1960s.
Complete the table below to explain your answer.
(4 marks)

Exam tip

Make two inferences and choose details from the source that directly support them. The examples below give only the first inference and support.

Average answer

What I can infer:
Some CCP officials lived in a very luxurious way.
Details in the source that tell me this:
The source says that 'They were cadres [officials] of high status.'

The inference is correct, but the detail used does not explain how the source shows that CCP officials lived in a very luxurious way.

Verdict

This is an average response because an inference is made, but without accurate support. Use the feedback to rewrite this answer, making as many improvements as you can.

Strong answer

What I can infer:
Some CCP officials lived in a very luxurious way.
Details in the source that tell me this:
The source refers to one official having 'deep soft sofas and armchairs, rugs, even a refrigerator'.

Details are given that support a correct inference.

Verdict

This is a strong response because an inference is made and supported from the source.

Paper 3, Section A: Question 2

Explain why Mao launched the Hundred Flowers campaign.
You may use the following in your answer:

- the first Five-Year Plan
- Mao's ideology.

You **must** also use information of your own.

(12 marks)

Exam tip

Focus on explaining 'why'. Aim to give at least three clear reasons.

Average answer

The Hundred Flowers campaign was a campaign launched by Mao in 1956. It was launched because of Mao's ideology. It allowed some people to criticise Mao, such as experts who Mao needed for his economics. At first Mao was happy about the criticism of people, and so the criticism carried on. Also, a writer called Liu Pin-yan wrote a book criticising the PLA. In the end, Mao stopped the Hundred Flowers campaign and launched the 'Anti-Rightist' purge.

The information here is accurate but too descriptive, and there is some detail about the way the campaign developed, but it is not directly linked to an explanation of why Mao launched the Hundred Flowers campaign.

Also, in 1956, workers went on strike because they wanted more pay. Mao thought the CCP was to blame for the strike. Mao wanted the workers to be free to say what they thought about pay and the CCP, because he was a communist who wanted the workers to have a say, so he decided to allow more freedom in the campaign.

Relevant information is given here and is additional to the stimulus points. However, it should develop this further with more specific detail, and by explaining how the actions of CCP officials explain the launch of the campaign.

The first Five-Year Plan was also a reason why Mao launched the campaign. The Plan led Chinese industry to boom. It grew at 16% a year from 1953 to 1957, exceeding targets in the production of coal and steel. The success of the Plan made Mao feel confident about the future.

Another reason for success is given here, which contains some accurate and relevant detail. However, the paragraph should develop the point fully by explaining why the success of the first Five-Year Plan led to the launch of the Hundred Flowers campaign.

Verdict

This is an average answer because:

- information is accurate, showing some knowledge and understanding of the period, and adds a point additional to the stimulus (so it is not a weak answer)
- it does not analyse causes explicitly enough to be a strong answer
- there is some development of material, but the line of reasoning is not clear.

Use the feedback to rewrite this answer, making as many improvements as you can.

Paper 3, Section A: Question 2

Explain why Mao launched the Hundred Flowers campaign. You may use the following in your answer:

- the first Five-Year Plan
- Mao's ideology.

You **must** also use information of your own.

(12 marks)

Strong answer

Mao launched the Hundred Flowers campaign for several reasons. The success of the first Five-Year Plan made him feel confident, strikes in 1956 made him worry that the CCP was losing touch and he was ideologically committed to giving workers and peasants a say.

Introductory sentence is not strictly necessary, but it sets out a series of clear reasons, and shows a strong focus on the question.

The success of the first Five-Year Plan led to the launch of the campaign. From 1953 to 1957, the Plan succeeded in building the foundations of modern industry, and the CCP completed major buildings like the Wuhan Yangtze River Bridge. This led Mao to launch the campaign because he believed the people would use their new freedom to praise the achievements of the Plan.

A detailed point, which clearly links to the question and provides a valid reason.

Mao was also worried about strikes. In 1956, workers stopped working in order to demand better pay, as the government had refused to give workers a pay rise in the first few years of the Plan. Mao was worried that the behaviour of CCP officials, such as corruption and inefficiency, was one of the reasons for the strike. Therefore, Mao launched the campaign to allow workers a say, so they could complain about CCP officials who were not doing their jobs properly.

The paragraph begins with a valid point, which goes beyond those given as stimulus. It backs this up with specific information, and ends with an explanation of its significance, tying the information to the question.

However, Mao's ideology was the most important reason for the launch of the Hundred Flowers campaign. Mao was a communist, and wanted workers and peasants to benefit most from society. However, he was worried that experts and CCP officials had more power and money than ordinary people. Mao was also worried that some of the bad things of Russian communism, like centralisation, would come to China because of the Plan. So, Mao launched the Hundred Flowers campaign because he wanted ordinary workers to criticise experts and stop them becoming too powerful.

The paragraph begins with the second stimulus point, which it supports with accurate relevant detail, and links to the other factors. Finally, it explains how ideology led to the launch of the campaign.

Verdict

This is a strong answer because:

- information is wide-ranging and precisely selected to support points that directly address the question
- the explanation is analytical and directed consistently at the question
- the line of reasoning is coherent and sustained.

148

Paper 3, Section B: Question 3a

For this section, you will need to use the sources and interpretations in the Sources/Interpretations Booklet (page 155).

Study Sources B and C.

How useful are Sources B and C for an enquiry into the status of women in China between 1949 and 1976?

Explain your answer, using Sources B and C and your own knowledge of the historical context.

(8 marks)

(page 155)

Exam tip

Consider the strengths and weaknesses of the evidence. Your evaluation must link to the enquiry and use contextual knowledge. Your reasons (criteria) for judgement should be clear. Include points about:

- what information is relevant and what you can infer from the source
- how the provenance (nature, origin, purpose) of each source affects its usefulness.

Average answer

Source B is useful because it tells you about marriage in China. It shows a woman and a man standing in front of a book. The book is the 1950 Marriage Law, and that explains why the poster is called 'Freedom of marriage', because the 1950 Marriage Law gave equal rights, ending things like dowries which made women inferior. The man and the woman also look equal as they are standing next to each other and both have rosettes and scrolls. It is a propaganda poster and so it showed things the CCP thought were important, and this source shows women's status around the time the Marriage Law was introduced.

Source C is useful because it shows that there was more than one view of the status of women. The writer says that men are still thinking in 'feudal or bourgeois' ways, showing that men are still not accepting women's equality. At the beginning, it implies that housework is not divided up equally, showing that in some ways women's status is not equal.

Source C is useful because it shows that the status of women was an issue for China. *Chinese Women* was a newspaper that gave advice the CCP thought was important to women. So Source C shows that women's status was important.

The answer contains a judgement about the usefulness of Source B which is related to the status of women, and is based on the content and provenance of the source. The paragraph begins to consider the source's context and its bearing on the source's utility.

Useful information is selected from the source to answer the question. The answer makes an inference from the source ('it implies that housework is not divided up equally'), but the inference is not supported by the content of the source.

This paragraph makes a valid statement about usefulness from the provenance of the source. The final sentence is also valid, but is not backed up by developed reasons.

Verdict

This is an average answer because:

- it has taken relevant information from both sources and shown some analysis by beginning to make inferences (so it is not a weak answer)
- it has added some relevant contextual knowledge and used it for some evaluation of both the sources, but this is not sufficiently developed
- it sets out judgements about the usefulness of the sources, but it does not base these on clear criteria. Therefore, it is not a strong answer.

Use the feedback to rewrite this answer, making as many improvements as you can.

Paper 3, Section B: Question 3a

Study Sources B and C.

How useful are Sources B and C for an enquiry into the status of women in China between 1949 and 1976?
Explain your answer, using Sources B and C and your own knowledge of the historical context. **(8 marks)**

Strong answer

Source B is useful as it gives an official view, from a government propaganda poster, of the status of women in China after the Marriage Law of 1950. It shows a man and a woman standing in front of a book containing the Marriage Law. The picture shows both wearing rosettes and both holding scrolls, so as they both have the same things, we can infer it is intended to show they are equal. The title 'Freedom of marriage' is useful as it could be a reference to the new rights that women won in the 1950 Marriage Law which abolished polygamy, child marriage and dowries, all of which made women inferior to men. However, the fact that the poster comes from 1953 could show that some women still did not know that they had new rights, as the poster appears to be designed to advertise the new rights. Therefore, in spite of it being propaganda, the poster is still useful because it suggests that women had new rights, but perhaps that not all women knew about them in 1953.

Source C is useful as it indicates that women's status was still not equal to men's. It says that some men's views of women are 'are not very correct' and still 'feudal'. Source C is likely to be accurate, as in 1963 the government had stopped using communal kitchens so that aspects of housework were more of a problem than they had been in the People's Communes.

Source C was published in Chinese Women. The magazine was not written to promote communism in other countries. It was written to give advice to women. Therefore, it could talk about real problems that women were having, such as men's old-fashioned attitudes and housework. It is useful for showing that women still had problems that were serious enough for the CCP to take seriously by encouraging women to 'struggle' with old-fashioned men to gain equality in the home.

> Good analysis of the evidence, and use of contextual knowledge to make inferences and interpret the source. A clear statement of utility is made.

> Strengths and limitations of the source are shown through inferences and an analysis of provenance and use of contextual knowledge. The judgements about utility are based on clear criteria.

Verdict

This is a strong answer because:

- it has analysed both sources, making inferences from them
- it has used contextual knowledge in the interpretation of both sources
- evaluation takes content and provenance into account and explains criteria when making judgements.

Paper 3, Section B: Questions 3b–c

Study Interpretations 1 and 2 on page 155. They give different views about the status of women in China between 1949 and 1976.

What is the main difference between these views?
Explain your answer, using details from both interpretations.
(4 marks)

Exam tip

Remember to identify a main difference and then use details from both interpretations to support your answer.

Average answer

A main difference is that Interpretation 2 says that women had an equal status to men, whereas Interpretation 1 says there were problems. For example, Interpretation 1 says there were problems with arranged marriages and unequal pay.

A valid difference is identified, but no details are given from Interpretation 2.

Verdict

This is an average answer because it identifies a difference, with some detail from Interpretation 1, but it does not use detail from Interpretation 2 to support the difference.
Use the feedback to rewrite this answer, making as many improvements as you can.

Suggest **one** reason why Interpretations 1 and 2 give different views about the status of women in China between 1949 and 1976.
You may use Sources B and C to help explain your answer.
(4 marks)

Exam tip

Give a clear reason. If you decide to use Sources B and C, choose details from them to show that the historians may have given weight to different sources.

Average answer

The interpretations may differ because the historians use different sources. Some sources, like Source B, imply that the Marriage Law led to equality in marriage. That supports Interpretation 2, which says that women had new rights and were allowed an equal share on farms.

A reason is given and Source B is used, but nothing is said about Interpretation 1.

Verdict

This is an average answer because it gives a reason for the different views with support from Source B, but Interpretation 1 is not considered.
Use the feedback to rewrite this answer, making as many improvements as you can.

Paper 3, Section B: Questions 3b-c

Study Interpretations 1 and 2. They give different views about the status of women in China between 1949 and 1976.

What is the main difference between these views?

Explain your answer, using details from both interpretations. **(4 marks)**

Strong answer

A main difference is that Interpretation 2 is very positive about the status of women. It emphasises the legal rights that women gained from the 'Marriage Reform Law' and from land reform. Interpretation 1 emphasises that in some ways women's status was not equal to men's. It focuses on the ways that the CCP's laws did not bring about change, for example, abuse of women and unequal pay were a problem.

Details from Interpretation 1 are used as well as those from Interpretation 2 to show the main difference between the views.

Verdict

This is a strong answer because it identifies the main difference with support from both interpretations.

Suggest **one** reason why Interpretations 1 and 2 give different views about the status of women in China between 1949 and 1976.

You may use Sources B and C to help explain your answer. **(4 marks)**

Strong answer

The interpretations may differ because they have given weight to different sources. For example, Source B, which contains a picture of the 1950 Marriage Law, implies that the CCP introduced new laws which gave women and men equal rights. This supports Interpretation 2, because it talks about the way laws helped improve the status of women.

Source C, however, gives support for Interpretation 1 because it implies that there are still some ways in which women's status is not equal to men's. Source C looks at the attitudes of men and the way housework is not divided equally. Rossabi may have used sources that refer to newspaper reports that women were still abused, and arranged marriages continued after the 1950 Marriage Law. These provide evidence for Interpretation 1, which focuses on the 'mixed' results of the CCP's law.

Details from Source B are used to show support for Interpretation 2 and details from Source C are used to show support for Interpretation 1.

Verdict

This is a strong answer because it gives a valid reason for the different views and supports it using both sources.

Paper 3, Section B: Question 3d

Up to 4 marks of the total for part (d) will be awarded for spelling, punctuation, grammar and use of specialist terminology.

How far do you agree with Interpretation 1 about the status of women in China between 1949 and 1976?

Explain your answer, using both interpretations and your knowledge of the historical context.

(20 marks)

Average answer

Interpretation 1 says that women's status was still not equal in China. It talks about abuse and 'unequal wages' and 'arranged marriages'. I know that men dominated the CCP as less than 13% of CCP officials were women from 1949 to 1965. Also, I know from my own knowledge that the CCP did not set up laundries or crèches as they wanted to spend money on industry.

But Interpretation 1 does not consider some parts of what the CCP did for women. The CCP used its power to end foot binding by the end of 1950. Foot binding was ended by the PLA, which enforced new laws about women across China. Also, it doesn't deal with women owning property. Land reform gave women property rights. Interpretation 2 shows that 'Women were allowed their equal share of the soil that they helped farm' after land reform. Interpretation 1 also doesn't talk about the way new laws affected female infanticide, which dropped from 10% in 1949 to 2% in 1960.
Overall, I do agree with Interpretation 1 that women did have an unequal status.

Relevant details are chosen from Interpretation 1 and own knowledge is included. However, the knowledge is simply added on to the extract. The answer should explain clearly whether the information supports or challenges the view.

Relevant details are chosen to contrast Interpretation 1 with Interpretation 2 and own knowledge is added in. A judgement is given, but this is not well explained.

Verdict

This is an average answer because:

- it has chosen relevant details from both the interpretations and used contextual knowledge in the answer, so it is not a weak answer
- it does not explain criteria for judgement clearly enough to be a strong answer
- spelling and grammar are accurate and there is some use of specialist terms such as 'land reform' and 'foot binding'.

Use the feedback to rewrite this answer, making as many improvements as you can.

Paper 3, Section B: Question 3d

How far do you agree with Interpretation 1 about the status of women in China between 1949 and 1976? Explain your answer, using both interpretations and your knowledge of the historical context. **(20 marks)**

Strong answer

Interpretation 1's view is that women never had an equal status to men in China between 1949 and 1976. To back this up, the interpretation refers to the CCP's media which reported 'arranged marriages and domestic abuse' as well as 'unequal wages'. There is also other evidence that shows that women never had equal status, such as prejudices of CCP and PLA officials, which meant they did not always take women's rights seriously. Also, men tended to demand that women did the vast majority of domestic work. This supports Interpretation 1's view that women did not have equal status to men, because it shows that men, including Party officials, did not respect some of their rights.

Interpretation 2 gives a different perspective. It argues that the Marriage Law and land reform changed the status of women massively, giving them equal rights to marry and to own land. There is evidence that women's status did improve due to the Marriage Law. For example, the number of child marriages fell by 85% between 1949 and 1965. Also, 76% of the divorces that were granted during 1951 were demanded by women. This supports Interpretation 2's argument that the law 'freed many women from subservient roles'. The PLA also made sure women gained property through land reform, and punished former landlords for mistreating women. Therefore, there is some evidence that women's status improved as they gained property and rights in marriage as a result of CCP laws.

Overall, both extracts show ways in which the status of women changed. Interpretation 2 is right that legal changes gave women a much higher status, and that many women made use of the new laws to gain greater independence. Interpretation 1 agrees that the Marriage Law of 1950 banned abuses such as female infanticide and arranged marriages. However, Interpretation 1 shows that the new laws were not totally successful, and abuse and inequality continued. Overall, I agree more with Interpretation 1 because, although there were clear improvements in women's status, the laws did not get rid of all inequalities.

Interpretation 1's argument is analysed. Relevant additional knowledge is chosen to support it, although this could be more specific.

Interpretation 2's argument is analysed. Additional knowledge is well used to develop the points from Interpretation 2.

A judgement is reached and both views are considered. Clear reasons are given to support the judgement. Spelling, punctuation and grammar are good, too.

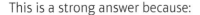

Verdict

This is a strong answer because:
- both interpretations are analysed and evaluated using own knowledge
- the line of reasoning is coherent and the judgement is appropriately justified with clear criteria
- SPaG demonstrates accuracy, effective control of meaning and the use of a wide range of specialist terms.

Sources/Interpretations Booklet

Source B

A poster, entitled 'Freedom of marriage, happiness and good luck', published by the CCP in 1953. The book in the background shows the first section of the 1950 Marriage Law.

Source C

From the Chinese newspaper *Chinese Women*, published in late 1963. The newspaper was published by the CCP and gave advice to women on how to live their lives.

Housework has to be divided up among the family and each person has to do some of it. It must not be overly concentrated on the female comrade. In this respect if the male comrade's thinking and views are not very correct and still include feudal or bourgeois remnants [old ways of thinking], the female comrade should not be overly accommodating and there is no harm in her carrying out a suitable degree of struggle.

Interpretation 1

From *A History of China* by Morris Rossabi, published in 2014.

The status of women was still another difficulty that the communists immediately tried to alter. The Marriage Law of 1950 forbade female infanticide, arranged marriages, domestic abuse, and discrimination against women in the labour force. The effects of the law in the early 1950s were decidedly mixed. The government-controlled press acknowledged the persistence of arranged marriages and domestic abuse as late as the 1960s. Communist media also documented unequal wages for women in many enterprises.

Interpretation 2

From *Mao Zedong's China* by Kathlyn Gay, published in 2007.

Another reform law focused on women and their status within marriage. ... Mao initiated the Marriage Reform Law of 1950, which freed many women from subservient roles. ...

Along with the new marital rights, women obtained new equality under land reform. Previously women had no right to own land, but the Agrarian Reform Law changed that. Men no longer held ownership of all the land. Women were allowed their equal share of the soil that they helped farm. ...

Women worked alongside men in factories and mills.

Answers to Recall quiz questions

Chapter 1

1. People's Liberation Army
2. 1946
3. Anything similar to: The working class or factory workers
4. Joseph Stalin
5. Around 2 million
6. The Huai–Hai campaign
7. Unemployment and inflation
8. Zhou Enlai
9. Beijing University
10. Anything similar to: A form of power, based on the ability to promote the careers of others.

Chapter 2

1. Mutual Aid Teams (MATs); Agricultural Producers' Co-operatives (APCs); Advanced Agricultural Producers' Co-operatives (Advanced APCs)
2. Anything like: Peasants could leave the Advanced APCs whereas membership of the communes was compulsory.
3. Key features include: provision of childcare and free canteens; long hours; each commune had its own militia; peasants did agricultural and industrial work.
4. Anything like: Mao wanted to make sure that Chinese agriculture and industry developed and he wanted the revolutionary will of the Chinese people to push forward economic development.
5. July 1959
6. Consequences include: The sacking of Peng Dehuai; encouraged senior CCP officials to lie about the success of the communes; delayed the recognition that the communes were failing; the launch of a 'second Leap'; the launch of the 'Anti-Right Opportunist Campaign'.

7. Reasons include: The success of the Soviet economy; the consequences of the Korean War; Soviet aid; Mao's desire to use resources efficiently; Mao's desire to create an industrial economy.
8. Heavy industry
9. Reasons include: Economic problems during the first Five-Year Plan; China's relationship with the USSR; Mao's ideology; Mao's desire to increase China's prestige; Mao's desire to use China's resources effectively.
10. Anything like: Pragmatism favours decisions and policies that will work, utopianism favours decisions and policies that are designed to create an ideal society.

Chapter 3

1. Tiananmen Square
2. Mao's reasons include: The power struggle inside the CCP; his desire to purify communism; the failure of the Socialist Education Movement; Mao's concerns about capitalist culture.
3. Policies that lead to capitalism rather than socialism
4. Liu Shaoqi and Deng Xiaoping
5. Attack the CCP
6. To purge Chinese culture of capitalist influences
7. 1969
8. In an aeroplane crash
9. 1973
10. Hua Guofeng

Chapter 4

1. Anything like: Hu Feng sent a report criticising the cultural policies of the CCP to the Central Committee.
2. Around 25 million

3. Customs include: Forced marriages; marriage of children; bigamy; men living with concubines; dowries.
4. Anything like: Having an appearance that is neither strongly male, nor strongly female.
5. Consequences include: Growth in the proportion of nuclear families; reduction of the proportion of extended families; men experiencing the 'three fears'; increased hardship for women as a result of the failure of the communes; eradication of female infanticide.
6. Anything like: Literacy rates improved from 20% in 1949 to 70% in 1976.
7. Improvements included: They educated people about hygiene; they educated people about family planning techniques; they provided basic medicines and first aid; they administered vaccines.
8. Reasons include: She understood Chinese culture as she had been an actress; she was a political radical; she wanted to reform culture in order to deal with her enemies in Chinese theatre; she wanted to reform culture in order to deal with political rivals.
9. The Patriotic Three-Self Church
10. Methods included: Banning specific religions; converting religious buildings into barracks and hospitals; closing, defiling or destroying religious buildings or religious objects; beating, imprisoning or killing monks, nuns and priests; propaganda campaigns; forcing foreign missionaries to leave; taking over religious schools and hospitals; banning traditional religious clothes; discouraging the celebration of traditional religious festivals.

Index

Acknowledgements

Picture Credits

The publisher would like to thank the following for their kind permission to reproduce their photographs:

(Key: b-bottom; c-centre; l-left; r-right; t-top)

Bridgeman Art Library Ltd: Pictures from History 50r, 58, 67, 68, 69, 70, Private Collection / The Chambers Gallery, London 90; **Getty Images:** AFP 47, 95, Bettmann 65, 113, Buyenlarge 21, ChinaFotoPress 46, Hulton Archive 126, Jack Birns 17, Jean Vincent 89, Jean-Philippe Charbonnier / Gamma-Rapho 122, Keystone 9, 24, 81, Keystone Features 133, Keystone-France 8, 25, 32, 42, 50l, Mark Kauffman 13, Photo 12 15, Richard Harrington 76, 87, Sovfoto 93, Sovfoto / UIG 104, 136, STR / AFP 97, ullstein bild 137, Universal History Archive 51, 86, VCG 7b, 77, 101, 110, 117, 130; **International Institute of Social History, Netherlands / IISH:** 27, Stefan R. Landsberger Collections 72, 98, 135, Stefan R. Landsberger Collections / Ding Hao / Shanghai People's Fine Arts Publishing House 63, Stefan R. Landsberger Collections / Niu Wen 115, Stefan R. Landsberger Collections / Revolutionary Committee of Sichuan Art Academy / Sichuan renmin chubanshe 128, 155, Stefan R. Landsberger Collections / Yu Yunjie (俞云阶) / Huadong renmin meishu chubanshe 121; **Magnum Photos Ltd:** Marc Riboud 64; **Mary Evans Picture Library:** 6, 14, 19, 30, 45, Everett Collection 82, Friedrich / Interfoto 7t, 80; **TopFoto:** Fine Art Images / HIP 123, The Granger Collection 105, World History Archive 116

Cover images: *Front:* **Mary Evans Picture Library:** Epic / PVDE

All other images © Pearson Education

We are grateful to the following for permission to reproduce copyright material:

Text

Extract on page 15, Interpretation 1, from *Edexcel as/A Level History, Paper 1&2: Communist States in the 20th Century Student Book + Activebook*, Pearson Education (Phillips,S.,Gregory,B.,Bushnell,N.) p.169, Pearson Education Limited ; Extract on page 16, Interpretation 2, from *China at War 1901–1949*, Routledge (Dreyer,E.L. 2014) p.350; Extract on page 16, Interpretation 3, from *The Chinese Civil War 1945-49*, Osprey Publishing (Lynch,M. 2010) p.70, © Lynch, M, 2010, The Chinese Civil War 1945-49, used by permission of Bloomsbury Publishing Plc.; Extract on page 17, Source F, from *Peking Diary*, Pennsylvania State University (Bodde,D. 1967) p.51, with permission from Taylor and Francis; Extract on page 25, Source D, from *The Private Life of Chairman Mao*, Random House (Zhisui Li 1996) p.56, Penguin Random House Group and Penguin Random House LLC with permission; Extract on page 25, Interpretation 2, from *Access To History: The People's Republic of China 1949-76 2nd Edition*, Hodder Education (Lynch,M. 2008) p.32; Extract on page 25, Interpretation 3, from *History+ for Edexcel A Level: Communist states in the twentieth century by Robin Bunce)*, Hodder Education (Bunce,R., Clements,D.,Flint,A. 2015); Extract on page 28, Source B, from Fanshen : a documentary of revolution in a Chinese village by HINTON, WILLIAM Reproduced with permission of UNIVERSITY OF CALIFORNIA PRESS in the format Republish in a book via Copyright Clearance Center; Extract on page 32, Interpretation 1 from *The Politics of China* (MacFarquhar,R. 1997) p.5; Extract on page 32, Interpretation 2, from *Mao's China and After* by Maurice Meisner. Copyright © 1977, 1986 by The Free Press, A Division of Macmillan, Inc. Copyright © 1999 by Maurice Meisner. Reprinted with the permission of Free Press, a Division of Simon & Schuster, Inc. All rights reserved; Extract on page 34, Interpretation 2, from *A History of China*, Wiley Blackwell (Rossabi,M. 2013) p.380, in the format Book via Copyright Clearance Center; Extract on page 34, Interpretation 3, from *Access To History: The People's Republic of China 1949-76 2nd Edition*, Hodder Education (Lynch,M. 2008) pp.36-37; Extract on page 35, Source C from *The Private Life of Chairman Mao*, Random House (Zhisui Li 1996) p.198, Penguin Random House LLC with permission and Penguin Random House LLC with permission; Extract on page 35, Source E from *The Writings of Mao Zedong, 1949-1976*, M.E. Sharpe (1992) p.301, The writings of Mao Zedong, 1949-1976 by KAU, MICHAEL Y. M., ; MAO, TSE-TUNG, ; LEUNG, JOHN K. Reproduced with permission of M. E. SHARPE INCORPORATED in the format Book via Copyright Clearance Center; Extract on page 37, Interpretation 4 from *Mao Zedong's China* Twenty-First Century Books (Gay,K. 2012) p.57; Extract on page 37, Interpretation 5, from Politics & purges in China : rectification and the decline of party norms, 1950-1965 by Teiwes, Frederick C. Reproduced with permission of M. E. Sharpe in the format Book via Copyright Clearance Center; Extract on page 46, Interpretation 1 from *Mao: A Very Short Introduction*, OUP (Davin, D 2013) p.56. By Permission of Oxford University Press; Extract on page 56, Interpretation 1, from *Food Security and Farm Land Protection in China*, World Scientific Publishing Co Pte Ltd (Yushi Mao, Nong Zhao, Xiaojing Yan), Unirule Institute of Economics, China, Food Security and Farm Land Protection in China, Yushi Mao, Nong Zhao, Xiaojing Yan, Copyright @ 2012 World Scientific Publishing Co. (WSPC); Extract on page 56, Interpretation 1, from *The People's Republic of China 1949-76*, Hodder (Lynch,M. 2010) p.69; Extract on page 52, Source D, from *Forgotten Voices of Mao's Great Famine, 1958-1962: An Oral History*, Yale University Press (Zhou, X. 2013) p.20; Extract on page 65, Source E, from A mood of caution, *Times* p.11, Wednesday, Jun 05, 1957; Extract on page 65, Interpretation 1, from *China 1900-76*, Heinemann (Stewart,G. 2006) p.99, Pearson Education Limited ; Extract on page 66, Interpretation 2 from *Demystifying the Chinese Economy*, CUP (Justin Yifu Lin 2012) p.100, Cambridge University Press; Extract on page 69, Interpretation 3 from *Party vs. State in Post-1949 China*, CUP (Shiping Zheng 1997) p.94; Extract on page 73, Source G, from *Forgotten Voices of Mao's Great Famine, 1958-1962: An Oral History*, Yale University Press (Zhou, X. 2013) p.206,208; Extract on page 79, Source B, from *Mao's people: sixteen portraits of life in revolutionary China*, HARVARD UNIVERSITY PRESS (1 July 1990) (Frolic, B.M) B016YMF9O4, MAO'S PEOPLE: SIXTEEN PORTRAITS OF LIFE IN REVOLUTIONARY CHINA by; Bernard Frolic Cambridge, Mass.: Harvard University Press, Copyright © 1980 by; the President and Fellows of Harvard College.; Extract on page 86, Source B, from *Growing Up in the People's Republic: Conversations between Two Daughters of China's Revolution*, Palgrave Macmillan (Ye,W. ,Xiaodong,M. 2005), Palgrave Macmillan; Extracts on page 88, Source E and page 97, Source F, from *Mao's people: sixteen portraits of life in revolutionary China*, Harvard University Press (Frolic,B.M. 1980) pp.72-73, MAO'S PEOPLE: SIXTEEN PORTRAITS OF LIFE IN REVOLUTIONARY CHINA by; Bernard Frolic Cambridge, Mass.: Harvard University Press, Copyright © 1980 by; the President and Fellows of Harvard College; Extract on page 88,Interpretation 1 from *A History of China*, Wiley (Rossabi, M 2013) p.389 in the format Book via Copyright Clearance Center; Extract on page 94, Interpretation 1 from *The Cambridge History of China*, CUP (Twitchett,D. and Fairbank,J.K. 1991) pp.107,110; Extract on page 94, Interpretation 2, from *China Under Mao, a Revolution Derailed*, Harvard University Press (Walder,A.G. 2015) p.205-6, CHINA UNDER MAO: A REVOLUTION DERAILED by Andrew G. Walder, Cambridge; Mass.: Harvard University Press, Copyright © 2015 by the President and Fellows; of Harvard College; Extract on page 101, Interpretation 1 from *Party vs. State in Post-1949 China The Institutional Dilemma*, CUP (Zheng,S 1997) p.146; Extract on page 104, Interpretation 2 from Burying Mao : Chinese politics in the age of Deng Xiaoping by BAUM, RICHARD Reproduced with permission of PRINCETON UNIVERSITY PRESS in the format Book via Copyright Clearance Center; Extract on page 102,Source B, from *Mao's Children in the New China: Voices From the Red Guard Generation*, Routledge (Jiang,Y. ,Ashley,D. 2013) p.13; Extract on page 102, Source C from *Tempered in the Revolutionary Furnace: China's Youth in the Rustication Movement*, Lexington Books (Pan,Y. 2003) p.92; Extract on page 105, Interpretation 3, from *The Politics of China: The Eras of Mao and Deng*, CUP (MacFarquhar,R. 1997) p.291; Extract on page 124 , Interpretation 1, from *A History of China*, Blackwell Publishing (Rossabi,M 2014) p.376, A history of China by Rossabi, Morris in the format Book via Copyright Clearance Center; Extract on page 124 from *Mao Zedong's China*, Twenty-First Century Books (Gay, K. 2007) p.86; Extract on page 131, Interpretation 1, from *China's Sent-Down Generation*, Georgetown University Press (Rene, H.K. 2013) p.32; Extract on page 131, Interpretation 2, from *Governing Health in Contemporary China*, Routledge (Huang,Y 2015) p.51; Extract on page 138, Interpretation 1, from *The People's Republic of China 1949–76*, Hodder (Lynch, M 2008) p.108, Reproduced by permission of Hodder Education.